Existential Thought
and
Therapeutic Practice

An Introduction to
Existential Psychotherapy

Hans W. Cohn

Lond   lhi

First published 1997

Reprinted 2000

 SAGE Publications Ltd
6 Bonhill Street
London EC2A 4PU

SAGE Publications Inc
2455 Teller Road
Thousand Oaks, California 91320

SAGE Publications India Pvt Ltd
32, M-Block Market
Greater Kailash – I
New Delhi 110 048

British Library Cataloguing in Publication Data

A catalogue record for this book is available
from the British Library

ISBN 0 7619 5108 3
ISBN 0 7619 5109 1 (pbk)

Library of Congress catalog record available

Typeset by Mayhew Typesetting, Rhayader, Powys
Printed in Great Britain by Biddles Ltd, *www.biddles.co.uk*

Contents

For
JENNY

Preface

My aim in writing this book is twofold: I wish to present an overall framework for an existential-phenomenological approach to psychotherapy and at the same time show how such a framework affects the day-to-day practice of the therapist. This aim inevitably shapes the structure of the book – it demands an emphasis on certain aspects of the approach while other aspects are unavoidably neglected. A few initial comments on what this book sets out to do and what it regards as beyond its scope seem, therefore, appropriate.

First, throughout the book the existential-phenomenological framework is compared with the assumptions of psychoanalysis as originally proposed by Freud. Though these have, of course, been modified over the years, their basic ideas underlie most forms of psychodynamic therapy. It seemed useful to introduce a new framework by comparing it with one that is more familiar, particularly as the existential approach is in many ways, historically and theoretically, a response to psychoanalysis. Moreover, just as theory and practice are interwoven in psychoanalysis, existential thinking beomes manifest in the therapeutic situation.

Secondly, this is not a history of existential psychotherapy. Like psychoanalysis, existential psychotherapy presents itself in a number of different models. To refer to them all would obscure the purpose of this book.

The model I am introducing is based on the attempts of two Swiss therapists, Ludwig Binswanger and Medard Boss, to find a new foundation for the practice of psychotherapy in the philosophical concepts of Martin Heidegger. Heidegger had a profound influence on the thinking of a number of European philosophers, particularly on that of Jean-Paul Sartre and Maurice Merleau-Ponty. I think it would be fair to say that Heidegger, Merleau-Ponty and Sartre are the most distinct voices in what became the philosophical movement called 'existentialism' in Europe. Though their views differed in many ways, they share certain basic philosophical assumptions. It is their ideas that form the basis of what I call existential psychotherapy in this book.

Thirdly, in order to maintain a clear outline of such a new framework, I had to neglect certain interesting and important approaches which introduce variations and modifications, particularly as they often seemed to me to deviate significantly from the basic concepts of the European movement. Such deviations frequently lead to a rather imprecise and almost colloquial use of words like 'existential', 'ontology' and 'authentic' without paying attention to their meaning in the context of existential philosophy.

Thus I find it difficult to discern a consistent philosophical framework in the work of R.D. Laing, and it was probably not his intention to provide one. For example, in his most influential book, *The Divided Self*, he points out in a footnote that he is using the word 'ontological' not in a philosophical sense like Heidegger and Sartre but simply as an adjective derived from 'being'. However, he does not compare his usage with that of the existential philosophers, and he established with 'ontological insecurity' a term that has become very popular with some existential therapists but drifts philosophically in a vacuum. This example may explain why I would find the inclusion of an exposition of Laing's work, interesting and influential though it may be, confusing and misleading.

A few words also need to be said about my reluctant decision not to include the group of American existential therapists who in any history of existential psychotherapy would, of course, occupy a prominent place. Though they are in varying degrees influenced by European developments, they seem to me very deeply rooted in their own philosophical tradition in which humanistic and pragmatist elements play a decisive part. It would take a separate study to do justice to the relation between existential and humanistic aspects of American existential psychotherapy, and this book is not the plae for it. It must, however, be stressed that American therapists have made important contributions to many aspects of existential therapy, and that their books have a great deal to offer to anyone interested in this new therapeutic approach.

Notes

1. Throughout this book references to Freud's work are taken from the Standard Edition; where possible, the reference for the Penguin volume (volume number and page reference) is also provided.

2. Names, occupations and personal details of clients described in the illustrations have been changed in order to make identification impossible.

Acknowledgements

When I was writing this book I was teaching the theory and practice of existential psychotherapy to students at the School of Psychotherapy and Counselling at Regent's College, London. The Dean of the School at the time was Prof. Emmy van Deurzen-Smith, who all but single-handedly put this approach on the therapeutic map in this country, provided opportunities for its training and gave it academic respectability. I thank her for giving me the chance to gain the experience that finds its expression in this book.

I also thank my students over a number of years whose questions and comments kept my mind open. Furthermore, I think with gratitude of the many stimulating talks with my colleague Ernesto Spinelli. My special thanks go to Sarah Young, who not only generously offered to prepare my manuscript for publication but also made numerous helpful suggestions.

Above all, however, I thank my friend Jenny Hay without whom this book would not have been written. She suggested it in the first place, helped it through its various stages in many searching discussions, never lost her belief in it in the face of all my doubts, and was throughout unfailingly encouraging. This book is dedicated to her.

1

What is Existential Psychotherapy?

Most forms of psychotherapy and counselling, unless they use a behavioural approach, keep within a framework derived from psychoanalytic concepts. Frequently, of course, these therapeutic approaches do not comply with the classical Freudian model – clients are not seen four or five times a week and a chair facing the therapist usually takes the place of the couch. The model of thought supporting the therapeutic process is, however, a more or less modified version of assumptions which are essentially psychoanalytic.

What is the core of these psychoanalytic assumptions? Freud suggested that 'instinctual' wishes which are experienced as threatening and unacceptable are 'repressed' into an 'unconscious' area of the psyche. Defences are built to prevent their return. When they try to re-enter consciousness, they do so in disguise. Such disguised wishes appear as dreams, as symptoms and as various forms of disturbed behaviour. The psychoanalytic process is, so to speak, a de-masking of disguised desires so that they can be accepted into consciousness and the need for disguise becomes redundant. The disappearance of symptoms and disturbances depends on 'making the unconscious conscious'. 'Where id was,' said Freud, 'there ego shall be' (1933: 80 [2: 112]). This account is of course over-simplified, but I think it contains the essence of a psychoanalytically informed therapeutic process.

More recently the term 'psychoanalytic psychotherapy' has been introduced to describe an approach that bases itself on the Freudian model. But I consider that all therapeutic approaches that call themselves 'psychodynamic' have their roots in psychoanalysis. The term 'psychodynamic' is often used very loosely but the word itself supports Walrond-Skinner's definition of psychodynamic as 'relating to a theory of interacting mental forces, operating within the psyche' (1986: 275), particularly if this interaction takes place unconsciously. This definition would apply to most forms of psychodynamic therapy, including Jung's 'analytical psychology'.

A number of theorists have seen psychoanalysis as an essentially biological speculation, concerned with 'instincts and their vicissitudes', as the title of one of Freud's papers puts it. ('Instinct' is in fact a mistranslation of the German word *Trieb* which means 'drive', a much less rigidly defined, more flexible concept than instinct.) In his *Three Essays on the Theory of Sexuality*, Freud described drives as 'lying on the frontier between the mental and the physical' (1905: 168 [7: 83]). Laplanche and Pontalis refer to them as representatives 'sent into the psyche by the soma' (1973: 215). Psychoanalytic theory is based on an exploration of the fate of these essentially biological forces, their origin, aims and 'objects'.

It was important for Freud to define psychoanalysis as a science. His own background was, of course, scientific: he studied zoology before he established himself as a neurologist and worked at the Viennese Physiological Institute under E.W. von Brücke, who believed that the natural sciences could provide the proper framework for the investigation of the human mind. Brücke's influence on the development of Freud's ideas cannot be over-estimated. Freud recognized that his propositions were extraordinary and sometimes shocking, and he realized the framework of the natural and physical sciences was likely to give them credibility. Apart from this, scientific terminology seemed to offer the possibility to put his discoveries into words. Thus his presentation of psychoanalytical theory used the language of the natural and physical sciences. Freud described the mind as a 'psychical apparatus', which is 'extended in space' and 'made up of several portions' (1940: 145 [15: 376]). This apparatus is kept in motion by a 'psychic energy' and functions through the interaction of its parts. Terms like projection, introjection and transference are derived from physics, and describe psychological change and interchange as if they were movements of matter in space.

Freud at times confessed that he was not at ease with his terminology. In his *Introductory Lectures on Psycho-Analysis*, after describing consciousness and the unconscious as two rooms with a threshold between them on which a 'watchman performs his function' and 'acts as a censor', he points out that these ideas are admittedly 'crude' and 'incorrect' and promises that he has 'something better to take their place' (1917: 295-6 [1: 337]). But he never revealed what this was, and the psychoanalytical vocabulary has remained essentially unchanged.

Though he presented psychoanalysis as a science, he was aware and regretted that his theories lacked predictability and thus fell short of classical scientific criteria. More importantly, he was concerned with meaning and thus stepped outside the aims of the usual scientific project with its concern for explanation and origin. Some dimensions of Freud's thinking fractured the Newtonian framework within which he tried to express it.

In the course of time - and more than a hundred years have passed since psychoanalytic ideas were first formulated - some psychoanalytic therapists and theorists have found the Freudian model too mechanistic and restricted to account for the wide range of phenomena met in the consulting room. The Freudian concepts seemed inadequate for an understanding of what was going on in relationships between people, and modifications and new conceptualizations seemed necessary to do justice to therapeutic experience.

W.R.D. Fairbairn laid the foundation of what he calls an 'object relations theory of the personality'. Fairbairn turned his back on the concept of instinctual energy. Though he retained the term 'libido', he defined it as 'object-seeking' rather than 'pleasure-seeking'. Further, he saw its aim in the establishment of relationships rather than the relief of tension. A number of psychoanalysts developed this new model, but though it focuses on relationships, these were brought about by the internalization of 'objects' - aspects and representations of other people. The model remained intrapsychic and did not explore what really happened between one particular person and another. D.W. Winnicott, for instance, was unwilling to examine the mother-child relationship only in the light of this theory and placed particular emphasis on what was happening between a child and its real mother. John Bowlby similarly regretted the loss of reality which followed the enthronement of intrapsychic fantasy at the centre of psychological happening. S.H. Foulkes, the creator of group analysis, saw the individual as an 'abstraction': he emphasized the priority of the group and described communication as the therapeutic process *par excellence*. His revision of psychoanalytical theory was quite radical and became the basis for group-analytic therapy; this will be discussed further in a later chapter.

Most therapists and theorists who felt dissatisfied with the theoretical framework offered by psychoanalysis either modified the meaning of its terms or integrated, with varying success, new concepts into the existing theory. Only a few attempted to refer their therapeutic experience to a new conceptual framework in order to see more clearly what had eluded previous explanations. Two therapists who did just this were the psychiatrist Ludwig Binswanger and the psychoanalyst Medard Boss. Both developed an existential-phenomenological – that is a philosophical rather than a scientific – approach to psychotherapy. They both called their approach *Daseinsanalyse* (literally, the analysis of being there), basing it on Martin Heidegger's philosophy of existence, though their understanding of what that meant differed considerably, as we shall see.

In my view, Binswanger's and Boss's work and writings are the most comprehensive and radical attempts made so far to provide a philosophical answer and alternative to Freud's scientific project. Binswanger was introduced to Freud by Jung, and his friendship with Freud survived their theoretical disagreements. At first, Binswanger tried to integrate Freudian ideas into his own approach, which was influenced by his studies of Husserl and Heidegger. However, in an important address on the occasion of Freud's eightieth birthday in 1936, Binswanger showed his dissent from Freud's approach very clearly. 'Now that he had developed his own anthropology on Heideggerian foundations, Freud's "naturalism" in the shape of man as homo natura, i.e. as being definable completely in terms of the natural sciences, proved in its one-sidedness to be unacceptable to Binswanger.' (Spiegelberg, 1972: 198–9).

Boss also had a personal contact with Freud – when he was 22 years old he was analysed by him, and this was the beginning of his training as a psychoanalyst. In his interesting 'self-presentation', Boss describes his early reservations about some of Freud's concepts, particularly his determinism and his dream theory, and the impact which Binswanger's address in 1936 had made on him:

> This excellent critique of Freud made me understand why Freud saw himself compelled to invent his dream theory

including his proposition of an 'unconscious'. As a child of his time he believed he had to submit to the rule of scientific dogma of a causal chain without gaps – a dogma he had taken over without question. (Pogratz, 1973: 87/8 – my translation)

It was also Binswanger who mentioned Heidegger's *Being and Time* to Boss. Boss felt he needed Heidegger's help to understand it; he wrote to Heidegger, and this led to a friendship that lasted many years. For fifteen years Heidegger visited Boss to run seminars in Boss's house for psychiatric students and colleagues. In 1987 a book appeared edited by Boss, the *Zollikoner Seminare*, which contains the summaries of ten years of seminars as well as the contents of many talks between Heidegger and Boss and excerpts from letters (this book remains untranslated). Also it is said that Heidegger co-operated in the writing of Boss's *Existential Foundations of Medicine and Psychology* (1979), though he is not mentioned as a co-author. Boss's conception of existential psychotherapy, which he presented in his 1963 book *Psychoanalysis and Daseinsanalysis*, is thus the result of a dialogue of many years between a psychoanalyst and one of the originators of 'existentialism'. Similarly, though less personally, Binswanger's new way of looking at 'mental illness' was the result of a continuing confrontation between Freudian concepts and the phenomenological explorations of Husserl and Heidegger. I do not think that any presentation of an existential psychotherapy can afford to neglect the extensive groundwork of Boss and Binswanger.

There is a significant difference in the approaches of these two Swiss pioneers in existential psychotherapy. There are a number of reasons for this. As a psychiatrist, Binswanger focused in his writings on the phenomenological investigation of the 'psychoses', that is, schizophrenia and manic-depressive afflictions. Boss also wrote about psychotic disturbances, but as a psychoanalyst he had probably a wider experience of the neuroses. Though Binswanger's ideas about therapy are implicit in his phenomenological descriptions, Boss concerned himself more openly with therapeutic questions. Most importantly, Binswanger was mainly influenced by the writings of Husserl and the early Heidegger, while at the time of Boss's closer contact with Heidegger the philosopher had, to some extent, left behind the more phenomenological aspects of *Being and Time*. It would be fair to say that we go to Binswanger for his subtle and often profound phenomenological descriptions of a client's world, while for our understanding of the therapeutic process, in the light of Heidegger's analysis of existence, we turn to Boss. In our exposition of the philosophical background we shall discuss this difference in greater depth.

Saying that we should not neglect the groundwork of Binswanger and Boss does not mean, of course, that this work is a kind of theoretical system to which we have to adhere. This would be a contradiction of the existential striving for openness to whatever addresses us. 'Daseinsanalysis' is, I think, a necessary point of departure but we need to go beyond it, as there are aspects of psychotherapy which have not been covered, or not covered adequately, by Binswanger and Boss. For an understanding of our relation to our body we need to turn to Merleau-Ponty, whom Heidegger is said to have praised for his insight into this problematic area. The question of groups has been raised by Sartre, but his interest is essentially political. In order to gain a phenomenological perspective on groups we need to consult Foulkes, though he never mentions phenomenology or existentialism. Finally, when it comes to the theme of sexuality Boss has left us with some ideas which are rather questionable and certainly not existential-phenomenological – in this area a great deal of work remains to be done.

This book, after a brief introduction to the basic concepts of existential phenomenology, outlines an existential-phenomenological approach to psychotherapy by comparing psychoanalytic and existential concepts. This will, I hope, revive something of the creative confrontation with Freud which characterizes the work of Binswanger and Boss.

References

Boss, M. (1963) *Psychoanalysis and Daseinsanalysis*. Tr. J. Needleman. New York: Basic Books.

Boss, M. (1979) *Existential Foundations of Medicine and Psychology*. Tr. S. Conway and A. Cleaves. Northvale: Jason Aronson.

Freud, S. (1905) *Three Essays on the Theory of Sexuality*. S.E. VII. London:

Hogarth Press. (Pelican Freud Library. Vol. 7. Harmondsworth: Penguin Books.)

Freud, S. (1917) *Introductory Lectures on Psycho-Analysis*. S.E. XVI. London: Hogarth Press. (Pelican Freud Library. Vol. 1. Harmondsworth: Penguin Books.)

Freud, S. (1933) *New Introductory Lectures on Psycho-Analysis*. S.E. XXII. London: Hogarth Press. (Pelican Freud Library. Vol. 2. Harmondsworth: Penguin Books.)

Freud, S. (1940) *An Outline of Psycho-Analysis*. S.E. XXIII. London: Hogarth Press. (Pelican Freud Library. Vol. 15. Harmondsworth: Penguin Books.)

Heidegger, M. (1987) *Zollikoner Seminare. Protokolle – Gespräche – Briefe*. Ed. M. Boss. Frankfurt a.M.: Klastermann.

Laplanche, J. and Pontalis, J.B. (1973) *The Language of Psychoanalysis*. London: Karnac Books.

Pogratz, I.J. (1973) *Psychotherapie in Selbstdarstellungen*. Bern: Huber.

Spiegelberg, H. (1972) *Phenomenology in Psychology and Psychiatry. A Historical Introduction*. Evanston: Northwestern University Press.

Walrond-Skinner, S. (1986) *A Dictionary of Psychotherapy*. London: Routledge & Kegan Paul.

2

Philosophical Background

Before we can turn our attention to an existential-phenomenological consideration of psychological phenomena we need to become familiar with some of the basic ideas of this philosophical approach. It is, of course, neither appropriate nor necessary to give a comprehensive outline, historically and conceptually, of this orientation. What I propose to do is to clarify those existential-phenomenological concepts which have a direct bearing on the phenomena and experience of psychotherapy. Besides, existential phenomenology is not a consistent 'system' which we have to accept in all its aspects and ramifications. Different existential philosophers and therapists vary in the emphasis they give to different dimensions of man's existence, man's relation to the world and other people. We have already seen that Boss and Binswanger, though both influenced by Heidegger, tend to differ in their therapeutic viewpoint.

Nevertheless, there are certain fundamental views, with a variety of nuances, shared by philosophers and therapists who call themselves 'existential'. It is on these views that our considerations will centre in this introductory section. First of all, we need to consider phenomenology and existentialism separately, and then see in what way they relate to each other.

The aim of phenomenology

It is often helpful to consider the etymology of a word in order to comprehend its full meaning. The Greek word 'phenomenon' is derived from a verb meaning 'to appear, to come into the light'. 'Logos', on the other hand, is rooted in a Greek verb meaning 'to say'. As John Macquarrie, in his book on existentialism, formulates it: 'Speech articulates the phenomenon' (1972: 25). 'Speech' implies here exploration and understanding. 'What appears' does not mean 'mere appearance' – whatever appears is real: reality is here not a Kantian 'noumenon', an unknowable 'thing-in-itself' hidden behind the 'phenomenon'. Heidegger's definition stresses the accessibility of phenomena: 'We must keep in mind that the expression phenomenon signifies that which shows itself in itself, the manifest' (1962: 51). This implies a consciousness to which it shows itself and is another way of saying that consciousness and world cannot be separated.

This is a new position for consciousness to be in. Since the seventeenth century Western thinking has been dominated by Descartes's separation of mind from matter, the thinking subject from the world. In the course of his bold search for certainty Descartes found that all was doubtful except our capacity to find it so – that is, to think – and that thinking alone guaranteed our existence. This conviction Descartes expressed in his famous saying: '*Cogito, ergo sum* – I think, therefore I am'. The consequence of this separation was that the mind was incapable of immediate apprehension of the world. (Another aspect of this separation is the split between mind and body, to which we will return.) Descartes did not deny that an interaction between mind and world took place, but he never explained how this could come about except by divine intervention, unless you take seriously his suggestion that the pineal gland acted as a kind of mediator. What had been – intellectually – separated could not be put together again and the gulf between subject and world, or subject and object as it is often expressed, seemed unbridgeable.

It was Husserl, the originator of phenomenology as a philosophical approach to knowledge, who (basing his ideas on the work of his teacher Franz Brentano) showed up the error which led to this artificial split. Brentano, introducing his concept of 'intentionality', had pointed out that: 'Every mental phenomenon is characterized by . . . what we might call . . . reference to a content, direction toward an object . . . In presentation something is presented, in judgement something is affirmed or denied, in love loved, in hate hated, in desire desired and so on'. (Brentano, 1995: 88). In his *Cartesian Meditations* Husserl takes up this point, directly referring to Descartes's '*Cogito*', 'Conscious processes are also called *intentional*; but then the word intentionality signifies nothing else than this . . . property of consciousness: to be consciousness of something; as a *cogito* to bear in itself the *cogitatum'* (Husserl, 1960: 33). In other words, there cannot be such a thing as just thinking – thinking is always thinking of something, as loving, hating, judging is always directed towards something. Our consciousness is intentional, and the intentional arrow has a path and a target. Consciousness is open towards the phenomena of the world, and the phenomena show themselves in the openness of consciousness. Phenomenology's original task was the exploration of the 'intentional arc': its path – the *manner* of experience – and its *target* – whatever is experienced. The split was not so much healed as shown to be fictitious.

It is the aim of phenomenology to describe, as far as possible, the intentional experience as uncontaminated by foreknowledge, bias and explanation. The method to achieve this is the 'reduction' (*epoche*) – by suspending everything that is not actually experienced we are in immediate contact with the 'what' of our experience itself.

We shall see how and why this phenomenological approach is welcomed by existential psychotherapists. But we need also to say that there are aspects of Husserl's reduction – which he described in different ways at different times – that many existential psychotherapists cannot accept, just as they were not accepted by most existential philosophers. For Husserl also 'suspended' the question of whether the content of experience actually existed or not, and he declared it as the aim of his method to arrive at the 'essence' of the experience itself.

Existential therapists are less interested in essence than in the particular situation and, not surprisingly, they do not wish to suspend what most concerns them: existence. They would follow Sartre's proposition that 'existence precedes essence'. For Heidegger, as we shall see, the essence of being human was existence.

The view of existentialism

For Heidegger the most important question was: What is Being? He did not mean by this, What is your being or my being? but rather, What is Being as such? Heidegger calls this 'the basic question of metaphysics'. In his inaugural lecture at Freiburg

University he formulated it in the following way: 'Why are there beings at all, and why not rather nothing?' (Heidegger, 1977: 110). It is the Being of beings Heidegger is concerned with, and he does not only ask what it is but also why we neglect this question. For among all beings, human beings alone have a capacity to ask this question. In a postscript to his Freiburg lecture Heidegger wrote: 'Man alone of all existing things . . . experiences the wonder of all wonders: that there is being' (Spiegelberg, 1982: 347).

The literal sense of the word 'existence' is 'standing out'. The Heidegger scholar and translator John Macquarrie says of man 'that among all beings that may be observed on earth he stands out as the only one that not only *is* but takes over its being in awareness of who or what it is and of who or what it may become' (1972: 69). Heidegger distinguishes Being (*das Sein*) from whatever actually is (*das Seiende*). In German there are two different words to indicate the difference, in English the capital B is used to distinguish Being from beings. Human being, which alone among all beings is aware of Being and able to reflect on it, Heidegger calls *Dasein*. This is generally translated as 'Being there', but I prefer Pivčević's suggestion that we call it 'the there of Being', the 'place where Being discloses itself' (Pivčević, 1970: 110). (Some writers do not keep to the distinction between Being and being, but I will try to do so.)

Heidegger distinguishes between 'ontological' and 'ontic' enquiries. An ontological enquiry explores those intrinsic aspects of Being which are 'given' and unescapable. For example, none of us can choose where and to whom we are born; none of us can choose to live forever; none of us can choose not to choose. But each of us responds differently to these 'givens' of Being and creates his or her own specific world within the all-encompassing world of Being. An exploration of the specific individual ways in which each of us is in the world is called ontic.

Heidegger thinks that all human beings have a basic under-standing of the ontological aspects of Being but most of the time escape from them into their ontic concerns. In other words, the difficulties and challenges of existence as such are often experienced as the demands and pressures of our personal life.

Let us look at these ontological aspects of existence for it is these 'existentials' and our disturbed relation to them which, as the existential analyst Condrau points out, 'seem significant in the clarification of individual symptoms' (1992: 111). Heidegger does not give us a single neat table of 'existentalia' (Solomon, 1972: 209). Different authors emphasize different aspects of existence. Those most frequently mentioned are: being-in-the-world, spatiality, temporality, embodiment, mood, being-with-others, facticity ('thrownness') and mortality. In other words, human existence, *Dasein*, is always in the world, in space, in time, in the body, emotionally 'attuned' (*gestimmt*), intersubjective and limited by death. To this I would add that human existence is always sexual and necessitates choice. I propose to have a closer look at these qualities of existence.

Being-in-the-world With this expression Heidegger describes our inevitable involvement with all that is. (Heidegger calls this involvement '*Sorge*' which is usually, but not very adequately, translated as 'care'.) We do not enter the world, so to speak, from outside but are always part of it. This inseparable relation is implied by the three hyphens.

Being-in-the-world-with-others Relatedness is a primary state of being – we cannot choose a world without other people. However, we can choose how to respond to this primary relatedness – what is also called 'intersubjectivity' – we can concern ourselves with it or turn our back on it. Over-involvement and isolation are both responses to being-with-others.

'Thrownness' Another of Heidegger's expressions, this points at the limits of our control over existence. Our life is conditioned in many ways; from birth onwards we find ourselves in unchosen situations. They include what Heidegger calls 'facticity' – our past history which in itself cannot be changed though our response to it can.

Mortality The awareness of the inevitability of death is a prerogative of human beings. It is our ultimate limitation which we can deny or accept as an intrinsic aspect of the process of living.

The inevitability of choice 'Man is condemned to be free', as Sartre sees it (1948: 34) – all choices are risky as none can be guaranteed to be right. It is not possible to avoid choice as refusing to choose is a choice too. However, the freedom to choose is the root of our creativity, though it provokes anxiety. As Kierkegaard says, this anxiety is 'the giddiness of freedom' (1980: 61).

Embodiment   The Cartesian split between body and mind is the result of a process of thinking and not an experience. All being is both physical and non-physical. 'Man taken as a concrete being is not a psyche joined to an organism', as Merleau-Ponty puts it, 'but the movement to and fro of existence which at one time allows itself to take corporeal form and at others moves towards personal acts' (Merleau-Ponty, 1962: 88).

Sexuality   This seems to me as much an intrinsic aspect of existence as mortality or intersubjectivity – we are in the world as sexual beings and confront as such the same complex interplay between what is given and the responses we choose. Sexuality has been strangely neglected by existential thinkers, with the exception of Merleau-Ponty who says: 'In so far as a man's history provides a key to his life, it is because in his sexuality is projected his manner of being towards the world, that is, towards time and other men' (1962: 158). (In the original, the meaning is not 'a man's history' but a 'human being's history'!)

Space   If existence is 'being-in-the-world', it is 'spatial' – that is, part of a wider context to which it is related. But the space between different parts of this context is not measurable in feet and yards but is experienced differently at different times; what is close today, can be distant tomorrow.

Time   Similarly we are 'temporal', as we *are* our history, moving from birth to death. But this movement is not experienced as a linear one-after-the-other, as the hand of a clock moves from one moment to the next, but the past is carried along by a present that is already anticipating the future.

Mood   The full meaning of the German *Stimmung* is not expressed by the usual translation of 'mood' – 'attunement' is closer to the original. It describes the affective aspect of the experience of Being-in-the-world. It is important not to see this as a simple one-way reaction to the world – mood does not only respond to what it meets, it also discloses it. For example anxiety is not just a response to the fact of finding yourself 'thrown' into the world – it is through anxiety that you become aware of this thrownness.

Existential thinkers are concerned with these intrinsic dimensions of Being and our place within them. How do these concerns relate to a phenomenological approach?

Phenomenology of existence

Phenomenology and the existential view have in common a focus on immediate experience. But the existentialist is predominantly concerned with the experience of existence, while the phenomenologist tends to explore the process of experience as such, without being interested in whether what is experienced actually exists or not. Robert C. Solomon puts it somewhat differently by saying that in the existential approach 'it is not those experiences relating to knowing and reasoning that are the paradigm to be examined but rather the experiences of doing, participating and choosing' (1987: 160). If human existence is 'being-in-the-world', it means that there is a constant involvement with all there is – interaction is inevitable and detachment impossible. Thus most existential thinkers reject Husserl's phenomenological reduction: 'A man is not a detachable consciousness who can abstract himself from the world around him' (Solomon, 1987: 179).

We can say that the existentialist is as much concerned with the 'phenomenon', with what immediately presents itself, as the phenomenologist. But for the existentialist this phenomenon is existence itself and our place as beings capable of reflection in the total situation of Being. Thus existential thinkers reject Husserl's 'transcendental' move into a search for essences and his suspension of existence. A distinction was made between a transcendental phenomenology and an existential phenomenology. What does the word 'transcendental' mean in this context? As Hammond, Howarth and Keat (1991) suggest, it has two meanings. The extent to which phenomenology tries to make no presuppositions, to 'bracket' all pre-knowledge, theory and bias, it is always 'transcendental' because it 'transcends' our everyday 'natural' approach to the world. But Husserl went beyond this. He proposed to bracket the actual 'empirical ego' itself and replace it with a 'transcendental ego' which constitutes the world but 'is not itself part of that world, but rather is presupposed by it' (Hammond et al., 1991: 5). It is this step that existential philosophers rejected. In fact they wondered whether this could still be called phenomenology or whether it was a kind of transcendental idealism. Their own focus was upon the 'active engagement in the world by individuals exercising their capacity to make choices and "compare meanings"' (Hammond et al., 1991: 6).

All existential psychotherapy has a phenomenological dimension. But different writers and therapists give different emphasis to the phenomenological and existential strands of their approach. Also an emphasis on phenomenological aspects is likely to focus on the ontic dimension of a situation, while an emphasis on existential aspects will be more concerned with ontological relevance.

We have already referred to differences in the 'Daseinsanalysis' of Boss and Binswanger. The difference is to some extent due to the fact that in Boss's presentation of therapy, existential concerns and the influence of Heidegger's later thinking dominate, while for Binswanger some aspects of the phenomenological propositions of Husserl and of Heidegger's earlier work provide the main theoretical impulse. The distinction between the contributions of these two important founders of the existential approach to therapy is one of the themes of a recent book by the Swiss daseinsanalyst Alice Holzhey-Kunz (1994), and what follows takes some of her ideas into account.

Binswanger defines the aim of his approach very clearly:

Existential analysis [*Daseinsanalyse*] does not propose an ontological thesis about an essential condition determining existence, but makes *ontic statements* – that is statements of factual findings, about actually appearing forms and configurations of existence. In this sense, existential analysis is an empirical science with its own method and particular ideal of exactness, namely with the method and the ideal of exactness of the *phenomenological* empirical sciences. (May et al., 1958: 192)

Binswanger took Heidegger's concept of 'Being-in-the-world' as the theme of his approach. But his concern was not with the ontological aspects of Being, which confront us all, but with the specific ontic ways in which the individual is in the world – that is, in his or her world. Binswanger's phenomenological analysis concerns a person's 'world design' – but this design is not the answer to a person's experience or history; it is an 'existential a priori' which underlies experience and history.

The constitution of the world by a 'transcendental Ego' is, as we have seen, an aspect of Husserl's phenomenology, and the influence of Husserl's thinking on Binswanger is here clearly evident. But this is not the place to enter this philosophically very complex and much debated area. It may help us to see Binswanger's concept of a person's 'world design' as a part of his or her constitution, as innate. It is this innateness that makes the world design a priori and transcendental. This approach shows itself, in Binswanger's words, 'as an understanding of the various psychoses, neuroses and psychopathies as variations of the a priori and transcendental structure of human existence' (1955: 304 – my translation).

The therapeutic process is an exploration of the client's world design in its various dimensions – *Umwelt, Mitwelt* and *Eigenwelt*. Emmy van Deurzen-Smith translates these as physical, social and psychological dimensions, to which she adds an *Überwelt* or ideal dimension. In her book on existential counselling she devotes a chapter to the 'clarification' of the clients' 'world view', which she sees as an important part of the therapeutic process without, however, implying that this world-view is an 'existential a priori' (van Deurzen-Smith, 1988: 69 ff.).

Binswanger has been criticized by Heidegger and Boss for having neglected the person's relation to the ontological aspects of Being. Binswanger talks about the structure of *Dasein* but Heidegger uses this word specifically to indicate man's unique capacity to be a 'there' for Being. 'An *analysis* of Dasein which leaves out the reference to Being . . . is not an analysis of *Dasein*' (Heidegger, 1987: 236 – my translation). We may or may not agree that Binswanger ignored a central aspect of an existential approach. But we have seen that he made it perfectly clear that he was not concerned with ontology. A detailed phenomenological description and clarification of a client's way of being in the world seems, however, a valuable aspect of any existential therapy and is by no means irreconcilable with our careful attention to the client's response to the givens of Being.

The difference between the approach of Binswanger and that of Boss is characterized quite clearly by Holzhey-Kunz. For Boss the emphasis is on 'world' as the 'possibility for being (*das Seiende*) to show itself as being (*Seiendes*) and be perceived as such by us. The concept of "world design" is therefore avoided, and in its place we have "realm of openness", "realm of illumination" and "clearing" as synonyms for world' (Holzhey-Kunz, 1994: 34 – my translation). As *Dasein* it is our concern to keep world open so that Being can show itself. Different individuals do this in different ways 'but the difference does not depend on the qualitative difference of world designs but on the degree of openness and correspondingly the narrowness or width of the illuminated realm' (Holzhey-Kunz, 1994: 35 – my translation). The restriction of our capacity to keep the world open for what we meet and what addresses us can be innate or the result of an unsatisfactory upbringing. It manifests itself in what Boss calls 'modes of illness' which show 'impairment' in our relation to certain intrinsic aspects of Being – that is, embodiment, spatiality, temporality and mood. All these disturbances 'encroach on the possibility of realizing the basic ontological nature of human existence: freedom and openness toward other human beings and towards all the other beings encountered' (Boss, 1979: 223). We can see that it is the 'ontological nature of human existence' – the 'there' of our *Dasein*, in which the intrinsic aspects of Being can be reflected – that is the ground of our disturbances. When Boss talks about illness, he does not distinguish between physical and mental impairment. All disturbances are seen daseinsanalytically as a restriction of our ability to reach from our ontic individuality to our ontological concerns with aspects of Being.

Binswanger's and Boss's approaches are both phenomenological – a descriptive exploration of what we encounter. But while Binswanger is exploring ontic world designs without enquiring into their ontological relevance, Boss explores his clients' relation to the ontological dimensions of Being; this gives his approach a specific existential emphasis. But the ontological aspect of the exploration does not exclude the ontic. 'There are some things which every ontic understanding "includes", even if these are only pre-ontological', says Heidegger (1962: 360). These are the ontological aspects of Being – thrownness, Being-towards-death, embodiment, mood. *Dasein's* understanding is always ontic-ontological, even if the ontological is often hidden by the ontic. Both the ontic and the ontological are part of an existential-phenomenological approach to psychotherapy.

References

Binswanger, L. (1955) *Ausgewählte Vorträge und Aufsätze*. Band 11. Bern: Franke.

Boss, M. (1979) *Existential Foundations of Medicine and Psychology*. Tr. S. Conway and A. Cleaves. Northvale: Jason Aronson.

Brentano, F. (1995) *Psychology from an Empirical Point of View*. Tr. A.C. Rancurello, D.B. Terrell and L.L. McAlister. London: Routledge.

Condrau, G. (1992) *Sigmund Freud und Martin Heidegger. Daseinsanalytische Neurosenlehre und Psychotherapie*. Bern: Huber.

Deurzen-Smith, E. van (1988) *Existential Counselling in Practice*. London: Sage Publications.

Hammond, M., Howarth, J. and Keat, R. (1991) *Understanding Phenomenology*. Oxford: Blackwell.

Heidegger, M. (1962) *Being and Time*. Tr. J. Macquarrie and E. Robinson. New York: Harper & Row.

Heidegger, M. (1977) 'What is metaphysics?', in D.F. Krell (ed.) *Basic Writings*. London: Routledge & Kegan Paul.

Heidegger, M. (1987) *Zollikoner Seminare. Protokolle – Gespräche – Briefe*. Ed. M. Boss. Frankfurt a. M.: Klostermann.

Holzhey-Kunz, A. (1994) *Leiden am Dasein*. Wien: Passage Verlag.

Husserl, E. (1960) *Cartesian Meditations*. Tr. D. Cairns. Hague: Nijhoff.

Kierkegaard, S. (1980) *The Concept of Anxiety*. Tr. R. Thomte. Princeton, NJ: Princeton University Press.

Macquarrie, J. (1972) *Existentialism*. Harmondsworth: Penguin.

May, R., Angel, E. and Ellenberger, H.F. (eds) (1958) *Existence. A New Dimension in Psychiatry and Psychology*. New York: Basic Books.

Merleau-Ponty, M. (1962) *The Phenomenology of Perception*. Tr. C. Smith. London: Routledge & Kegan Paul.

Pivčević, E. (1970) *Husserl and Phenomenology*. London: Hutchinson University Library.

Sartre, J.P. (1948) *Existentialism and Humanism*. Tr. P. Mairet. London: Methuen.

Solomon, R.C. (1972) *From Rationalism to Existentialism*. New York: Harper & Row.

Solomon, R.C. (1987) *From Hegel to Existentialism*. Oxford: Oxford University Press.

Spiegelberg, H. (1982) *The Phenomenological Movement*. 3rd edn. The Hague: Nijhoff.

3
Existential Psychotherapy and Psychoanalysis: a Comparison

'What do we mean by saying that existence precedes essence?', asks Sartre. He continues, 'We mean that man first of all exists, encounters himself, surges up in the world – and defines himself afterwards' (1948: 28). 'Existence' is here opposed to 'essence', and I propose to use Sartre's saying as the starting point for an initial comparison between existential psychotherapy and psychoanalysis. I believe that such a comparison, though it cannot escape from being an over-simplification, will give an insight into the basic aspects of an existential-phenomenological approach to psychotherapy.

What does Sartre mean? To make his point he uses the old metaphysical polarization of existentia and essentia. The essence of something is its definition: there are an infinite number of different apples, but what is it that makes it possible for us to call them all apples, what is it that defines their 'appleness'? It is those features that they all have in common – their essence. Can we say the same of human beings? There are a number of features we can point to which enable us to call human beings 'human' – the gift of speech, for instance, or the upright posture. Sartre would not deny this. But he gave priority not to what all human beings have in common but rather to their individual uniqueness – to their existence, their 'being there'. When Sartre goes on to say that 'Man is nothing but what he makes himself', he does not mean that we can choose the circumstances of our life but that we are free to choose our response to them, and that it is this response that defines each of us.

It is in this sense that existential psychotherapy is concerned with existence rather than essence, with this man or woman rather than with 'man' in the generic sense. It does not ask 'what is man?' but rather 'how is this man or woman?'. It is less interested in the explanation of human behaviour than in the phenomenon of human behaviour as such.

Freud, in his *Introductory Lectures on Psycho-Analysis*, declares:

> We seek not merely to describe and to classify phenomena, but to understand them as signs of an interplay of forces in the mind, as a manifestation of purposeful intentions working concurrently or in mutual opposition. We are concerned with a *dynamic view* of mental phenomena. In our view the phenomena that are perceived must yield in importance to trends which are only hypothetical. (1916: 67 [1: 95])

The search for hypothetical trends is the search for explanations which are valid for all human beings, for 'man'. Freud's attempts to describe the structure of the mind; his outline of certain developmental phases through which we all had to pass; his discovery of certain conflicts – like the Oedipus complex – which each of us had to live through: these all served the purpose of constructing an explanatory system that would help us to understand the various aspects of human behaviour.

We can say, I think, that psychoanalysis is less concerned with individual existence than with common trends, what we might call 'essences'. On this concern psychoanalysis bases its claim to being a science. This is illustrated strikingly by a comparison between two attempts to describe what is generally called 'mind', one by Freud and the other by Heidegger.

Freud's description of 'mental life' is taken from his last attempt at summing up his ideas in *An Outline of Psycho-Analysis*:

> We assume that mental life is the function of an apparatus to which we ascribe the characteristics of being extended in space and of being made up of several portions – which we imagine, that is, as resembling a telescope or microscope or something of the kind. (1940: 145 [15: 376])

Heidegger's exposition was part of the first seminar he gave to therapists and students at the Burghölzli psychiatric hospital in Zurich:

> Human existence is essentially never just an object that is somewhere present, least of all an object closed in itself. Rather,

this existence consists of 'mere' potentialities to perceive and be aware of all that encounters and addresses it . . . this new 'ground' of human existence should be called *Dasein* or 'Being-in-the-world'. (Heidegger, 1987: 3 – my translation)

A comparison of these two quotations can tell us something about the difference between a psychoanalytic and an existential approach to what Freud calls 'mental life'. Freud has a concrete concept of the 'psyche'; he sees it as a kind of mechanism whose function depends on a balanced interaction between its parts. This image is, of course, a metaphor but metaphors often do not only represent reality – they are often mistaken for reality, particularly when the reality they represent is as elusive as the human mind. Throughout Freud describes psychic events as if they were mechanical – movements of matter in space; terms like 'projection', 'transference', and 'displacement' arise naturally from the basic metaphor he has chosen.

In Freud's description of the 'psychical apparatus' we hear an echo of Descartes's distinction between '*res extensa*' and '*res cogitans*'. For Descartes all matter was 'extended', and everything was 'matter' except the 'thinking I'. Thus the world was material, a 'machine' obeying mechanical laws; only the mind was un-extended, immaterial. It is interesting that Freud went beyond Descartes and turned even the mind into an 'apparatus'. Descartes would have found this unacceptable.

Heidegger does not speak of mind but of 'human existence' or *Dasein*, but he ascribes to it 'potentialities to perceive and be aware of all that encounters and addresses it', potentialities that we might consider to be 'mental'. The emphasis is here on the potential openness to perception and experience, but this openness is not located in an 'apparatus', 'an object closed in itself'. Such an approach makes it impossible to describe relational phenomena as if they were an exchange of 'objects' across a gap which divides one person from another. It denies the Cartesian split between subject and world.

In psychoanalysis, the concept of a structured psyche leads to the view of psychological disturbance as a structural flaw, an intrapsychic lack or loss of balance. If therapy wishes to bring about a change, this change will have to be intrapsychic – a change in the internal structure and equilibrium. If on the other hand human existence is seen as a potential openness to perception and experience – and that means both to perceive and experience and being perceived and experienced – then the disturbance occurs at the point where this mutual involvement of persons takes place, that is, in the world where our being is. It is there, in the in-between, that therapy can effect a change.

Having seen that psychoanalysis and existential therapy tend to define the place of disturbance differently, what about the nature of disturbance itself? First of all we see some common ground – for it seems to be always an unaccepted, disowned aspect of our being that is at the root of a disturbance. Whatever is disowned tends to return, often in disguise, and it is the warding-off of the return of what is disowned, the fear of facing the unaccepted, that forms the core of the disturbance. The difference lies in the nature of the unaccepted. In psychoanalysis it is unacceptable drives, wishes and desires that are 'repressed' into an area of the psyche which is called 'the unconscious'. When these drives, wishes and desires return from their hiding place, the defence against them can take the form of 'symptom formation'. This Freud saw as a compromise between the original wish and the repressing force. The wishes are thus disguised and perhaps rendered less fearful but the symptoms which have taken their place can be disturbing and painful, and lead the sufferer to the therapist. Therapy would then consist in the freeing of the wish from its disguise so that what was 'unconscious' can be made 'conscious' and integrated. The existential therapist proposes that it is unaccepted aspects of existence itself which are at the core of the disturbance. We have seen that human existence has certain intrinsic qualities over which we have no control – like mortality, the inevitability of choice, the unavoidability of other people. We are free to respond to these existentials – we can accept them or turn our back on them, drop them from our awareness (this would correspond to the psychoanalytic notion of repression). These unaccepted aspects of existence also reappear throughout our life and can be warded off in many ways – by denial, evasion and distraction (this might be seen as an equivalent of the psychoanalytic concept of 'symptom formation'). Existential therapy may see it as its aim to help its clients to free themselves from the disturbing consequences of denial, evasion and distraction by enabling them to change their response to the existential givens.

From the existential-phenomenological viewpoint the question of the capacity of human beings to relate does not arise, as human relatedness is a primary 'given'. Proceeding from the experience of 'Being-in-the-world' (Heidegger) we find ourselves always in the world with others, never as separate entities but defined by others, as we define them. I talk about relatedness rather than 'relationship', as the more common word implies certain qualities (good or bad) or a desirable state of being to be achieved. When we say that human beings are in a state of relatedness, that existence is relational, nothing is said about the quality of this relatedness. Isolation is also a state of relatedness characterized by a separation from others.

The view that the individual person is defined by his or her relational context is, of course, not an existential prerogative. Donald Winnicott's much-quoted saying that 'there is no such thing as a baby . . . if you show me a baby you certainly show me also someone caring for the baby', is making this very point, and his subsequent proposition that 'the centre of gravity of being does not start off in the individual, it is in the total set-up' (1958: 99), comes very close to a phenomenological formulation. Similarly Foulkes, a classically trained psychoanalyst, stated in his first book: 'Each individual – itself an artificial though plausible abstraction – is basically and centrally determined, inevitably, by the world in which he lives' (1948: 10). The priority of relational factors underlies his conception of therapy in groups, as we shall see.

This primacy of the individual's relational context, his or her always being-in-the-world-with-others, is often called 'intersubjectivity'. 'Phenomenologically, society is intersubjectivity', writes Laurie Spurling (1977: 86) in his sociological exploration of the work of the phenomenologist Merleau-Ponty. The existential-phenomenological emphasis on the totality of the lived situation rather than on an abstracted subjective aspect of it is expressed by Merleau-Ponty: 'True reflection presents me to myself not as an idle and inaccessible subjectivity, but as identical with my presence in the world and to others, as I am now realizing it: I am all that I see, I am an intersubjective field' (1962: 452).

It is perhaps necessary to stress that intersubjectivity does not deny the existence and uniqueness of the individual. It prevents the individual from being frozen into solipsistic isolation but also does not allow him or her to be swallowed up by systemic inter- action where the system is everything and the individual has disappeared. Intersubjectivity opens up subjectivities to each other and shows them to be always flexible and incomplete.

Consequences for therapy

On the assumption that we exist primarily in a state of related- ness, it would be meaningless to distinguish between a 'real' and a transference relationship. The therapeutic relationship is always real – it is what we are 'in', what we experience, and it is always mutual. It includes certain phenomena which psychoanalysts call transference, but these are part of its totality.

How can we understand these transference phenomena exis- tentially? We cannot use the image of 'projection', which, as Boss points out, presupposes '1) the existence of two thing-like "egos" or "psyches" and 2) the possibility of throwing some of the contents of one of these "psyches" over into the other' (Boss, 1963: 126). The existential view does not assume gaps that need to be bridged. We turn instead to an exploration of the way in which we enter new situations, new relationships, and we find that our present experience is inevitably informed (though not caused) by anticipations based on past experience. Is this not, in fact, how we experience anything? Perhaps we can say that the shape and direction of our experiential capacity is to some extent formed by past experience.

The existential concept of time sees past, present and future not in linear succession but as multidimensional. The past is still present in a present that anticipates the future. Merleau-Ponty (1962: 69) describes this succinctly: 'each moment in time calls all the others to witness'. Likewise John Richardson, in his book on existential epistemology, gives a lucid account of existential temporality: 'We reach ahead towards our ends, from out of a rootedness in what we have been and through . . . the activities with which we are preoccupied.' (1986: 94). Thus, a client will not 'transfer' his or her past experience of mother or father on to the therapist, covering up the therapist's reality in the process, but the way in which the client has experienced father or mother will enter his or her experiential approach to the therapist. This does not occur, as it were, as a leftover from the past, but as an aspect of the client's present capacity to experience a person of a certain kind – say a person in authority from whom help is accepted but whose intervention is also suspected and resented. That part of the therapeutic relationship is no less real than whatever else is experienced in it. The therapist's experience is similarly informed.

Saying that the therapeutic relationship is throughout real and mutual does not mean that the contributions the therapist and client make are the same. The therapeutic relationship has a task, and this task shapes the form the relationship takes. The task is the clarification of whatever the client brings to the session. The session provides the space in which the client talks and the therapist listens. The client talks about whatever she or he wishes to talk about; the therapist listens as carefully and unselectively as possible. The therapist also responds in other ways – by asking questions and/or making comments – but whatever the therapist's response, it is meant to serve the clarification of the client's concerns.

A closer look at the therapeutic relationship will introduce a more detailed characterization of an existential-phenomenological approach.

References

Boss, M. (1963) *Psychoanalysis and Daseinsanalysis.* New York: Basic Books.

Foulkes, S.H. (1948) *Introduction to Group-Analytic Psychotherapy: Studies in the Social Integration of Individuals and Groups.* London: Karnac.

Freud, S. (1916) *Introductory Lectures on Psycho-Analysis.* S.E. XV, London: Hogarth Press. (Pelican Freud Library. Vol. 1. Harmondsworth: Penguin Books.)

Freud, S. (1940) *An Outline of Psycho-Analysis.* S.E. XXIII. London: Hogarth Press. (Pelican Freud Library. Vol. 15. Harmondsworth: Penguin Books.)

Heidegger, M. (1987) *Zollikoner Seminare. Protokolle – Gespräche – Briefe.* Ed. M. Boss. Frankfurt a.M.: Klostermann.

Merleau-Ponty, M. (1962) *The Phenomenology of Perception.* Tr. C. Smith. London: Routledge & Kegan Paul.

Richardson, J. (1986) *Existential Epistemology: a Heideggerian Critique of the Cartesian Project*. Oxford: Clarendon Press.

Sartre, J.P. (1948) *Existentialism and Humanism*. Tr. P. Mairet. London: Methuen.

Spurling, L. (1977) *Phenomenology and the Social World. The Philosophy of Merleau-Ponty and its Relation to the Social Sciences*. London: Routledge & Kegan Paul.

Winnicott, D.W. (1958) *Through Paediatrics to Psychoanalysis*. London: Hogarth Press.

4

The Therapeutic Relationship

The therapeutic relationship is the interaction between therapist
and client, which according to most theories is central to the
process of psychotherapy. In order to present the existential-
phenomenological view of the therapeutic relationship, I shall
compare it with the concepts of transference and countertransference. These two notions define the psychoanalytic understanding of the therapeutic process.

The psychoanalytic view

Transference

To the psychoanalyst, the therapeutic relationship is dominated
by a process called 'transference'. What is being transferred? In
Freud's words, it is 'a transference of feelings on to the person
of the doctor', when it is unlikely 'that the situation in the
treatment could justify the development of such feelings'.
Freud suggests 'that the whole readiness for these feelings
is derived from elsewhere, that they were already prepared in
the patient and, upon the opportunity offered by the analytic
treatment, are transferred on to the person of the doctor' (1917:
442 [1: 494]).
How does the analyst deal with this process? Freud explains:

> We overcome the transference by pointing out to the patient
> that his feelings do not arise from the present situation and do
> not apply to the person of the doctor, but that they are repeating
> something that happened to him earlier. In this way we oblige
> him to transform his repetition into a memory. (1917: 443–4
> [1: 496])

At this point the therapeutic importance of the transference becomes clear. Freud states:

> We must not forget that the patient's illness . . . is not something which has been rounded off and become rigid but that it is still growing and developing . . . what happens is that the whole of his illness' new production is concentrated upon a single point – his relation to the doctor . . . All the patient's symptoms have abandoned their original meaning and have taken on a new sense which lies in a relation to the transference . . . But the mastering of this new, artificial neurosis coincides with getting rid of the illness which was originally brought to the treatment – with the accomplishment of our therapeutic task. (1917: 444 [1: 497])

In other words, the 'new artificial neurosis' which Freud calls 'transference neurosis' offers the opportunity to free the patient from the symptoms which brought him or her into therapy in the first place. Thus, without 'transference' there can be no successful therapy. This also explains why in Freud's view sufferers from 'narcissistic neurosis' (essentially the psychoses) could not be reached by psychoanalysis; they have no capacity for transference.

There is a copious literature on this process, and there have been many variations on the original notion with shifting emphasis on one aspect or another. It is generally admitted that transference phenomena are not limited to the psychoanalytic situation. But the development of the transference is thought to be stronger and more easily observed in psychoanalysis, particularly when the analyst remains impersonal and unknown, and thus encourages the transfer of significant figures of the past.

Some psychoanalysts believe that it is mainly, or only, transference interpretations which bring about the required change in the patient. Melanie Klein, under the influence of her experience with small children who re-enacted their current phantasies in the analytic session, redefined the concept of transference. 'The practice of Kleinian psychoanalysis has become an understanding of the transference as an expression of unconscious phantasy, active right here and now in the moment of analysis. The transference is, however, moulded upon the infantile mechanisms with which the patient managed this experience long ago.' (Hinshelwood, 1989: 449). What is transferred here are infantile mechanisms rather than significant figures from childhood. One might wonder whether this process can still be called transference; it seems only loosely connected with Freud's original concept.

Countertransference

Freud introduced the term 'countertransference' in a talk entitled *The Future Prospects of Psycho-Analytic Therapy* at the Nuremberg International Psycho-Analytic Congress in 1910. When discussing the physician's experience he says: 'We have become aware of the "counter-transference", which arises in him as a result of the patient's influence on his unconscious feelings, and we are almost inclined to insist that he shall recognize this counter-transference in himself and overcome it.' (Freud, 1910: 144–5). It was this possibility of counter-transference which eventually led to the requirement of a training analysis.

Freud refers to counter-transference on only one other occasion, in his *Observations on Transference-Love* (1915). He discusses a patient's inclination to fall in love with her analyst and adds: 'For the doctor the phenomena signifies . . . a useful warning against any tendency to a counter-transference which may be present in his own mind. He must recognize that the patient's falling in love is induced by the analytic situation and is not to be attributed to the charms of his own person' (Freud, 1915: 160–61). It is often forgotten – not surprisingly as it does not quite tally with the meaning generally given to the concept of transference – that in this paper Freud also emphasized that: 'We have no right to dispute that the state of being in love which makes its appearance in the course of analytic treatment has the character of a "genuine" love' (1915: 168).

Freud clearly saw countertransference as an obstacle to therapy. A different concept of it was suggested by Paula Heimann in a paper she read at a Psychoanalytical Congress in Zurich in 1949. In it she regrets that Freud's images of the analyst as a surgeon, or a mirror, seem to exclude the analyst's feelings. Instead Heimann proposes the use of the term countertransference 'to cover all the feelings which the analyst experiences towards his patient' (Heimann, 1989: 74). She thinks 'that the analyst's emotional response to his patient . . . represents one of the most important tools for his work. The analyst's countertransference is an instrument of research into the patient's unconscious' (1989: 74). Clearly influenced by Klein's notion of 'projective identification' – she was still a Kleinian when she wrote this paper – Heimann describes this 'research into the patient's unconscious' most vividly: 'The analyst's countertransference is not only part and parcel of the analytic relationship, but it is the patient's *creation*, it is part of the patient's personality' (1989: 77). What we meet here is a version of the Kleinian belief that an aspect of the patient can be 'projected' into the analyst.

This paper, short though it is, proved important and controversial. Some psychoanalytic psychotherapists think that calling 'all the feelings the analyst experiences towards his patient' countertransference is broadening the term so much that it tends to become meaningless. Others welcome the extension and feel that it will open up new areas of insight and interpretation.

The 'real' relationship

In the psychoanalytic view of the relationship, the emphasis is on transference and countertransference but there remains also a place for the 'real' relationship between analyst and patient, though this place is not very clearly defined. Some psychoanalysts see the real relationship emerging as the transference is being dismantled. Others stress the importance of a 'working alliance', a 'realistic co-operation and collaboration in the therapeutic process' (Moore and Fine, 1990: 195), as a condition for a successful therapy.

But the question arises whether this is just another way of speaking about a positive transference, which Freud originally thought indispensable for psychoanalysis, or whether we talk about 'relationship factors' which are 'distinguishable from the techniques that [the therapist] uses or the theory upon which they are based' (Walrond-Skinner, 1986: 295), and should thus remain outside analysis.

The existential-phenomenological approach

The relational view of the therapeutic situation

We have seen, in our comparison between psychoanalysis and existential psychotherapy, that the assumption of a primary relatedness – an inevitable involvement of human beings with each other – rules out the Freudian concept of transference. The client's as well as the therapist's experience of each other will, of course, also be informed by previous experiences of significant persons, but this does not make the client–therapist experience any less real, though it may make it less transparent and thus in need of clarification. Phenomenologically, there is no distinction between a real and a transference relationship. The therapeutic relationship is always real but – as all reality – in need of elucidation.

We have also seen that within this real and mutual relationship, the contributions of client and therapist are necessarily different. Both are concerned with clarification – but it is the clarification of the client's story. In the following sections we shall explore the therapist's specific contribution to this clarification – in the form of observation, interpretation, and the creation of a space in which the client's story can be heard.

The first session

Within the framework of an existential-phenomenological understanding, there are some aspects of the therapist's first meeting with a client which deserve consideration:

1 The client you meet as the therapist is the client who meets you. There is no client *as such*. If two therapists meet the same client, it is not the same client.
2 What the client tells you as the therapist, she or he tells only you. She or he may tell another therapist something quite different.
3 There is no 'history' to be taken for there is no history *as such*. A client's history is disclosed in the process of interaction between therapist and client.

4   This means that there cannot be an 'assessment' as this would
    imply an objective situation independent of time, place and
    the contribution of the assessing therapist.

These considerations arise from the existential emphasis on
context, and the distortion and falsification which follow any
attempt to isolate any particular aspect from the total situation of
which it is a part. At times it will be difficult, if not impossible, to
act on these considerations – assessment and history-taking are
part of most therapeutic work in the public sector – but it is
important to keep their limitations in mind.

It is in our first meeting with a client that a phenomenological
approach can be particularly helpful, keeping in mind the three
'rules' which Spinelli outlined in *The Interpreted World* (Spinelli,
1989: 17 ff.): the rules of *epoche*, description and equalization.

The rule of epoche   The Greek word *epoche*, one of the basic
terms of Stoic philosophy, means 'suspension of belief', and in the
context of phenomenology it implies the 'bracketing' of our
assumptions, prejudices and expectations when facing our
experience.

When meeting a client for the first time, we often already
know something about him or her, particularly when the client
has been referred to us by another therapist, general practitioner
or psychiatrist. Whatever we know or are being told will turn
our minds towards previous experiences or theories. Referral
notes will trigger off a whole chain of thoughts and anticipations.
By the time we actually meet the client we are likely to be full of
ideas about the nature of his or her difficulties and our own
feelings about them. All this the rule of *epoche* asks us to
'bracket', so that our experience of the client can be immediate
and unbiased. This 'bracketing' can never be complete, of
course, but it is important to remember the pitfalls of pre-
knowledge and prejudgement.

The rule of description   This rule can be briefly summed up as,
in the words of Spinelli, 'Describe, don't explain'. It emphasizes a
careful examination of all that shows itself without rushing, as we
often do, from description to explanation.

What shows itself in a therapeutic session – the phenomena
that are experienced – is a total situation, including the therapist

but also the time of the session and the space in which it happens. Again the observation cannot be complete but the fuller it is, the more it is likely to do justice to what is going on.

The rule of equalization   This rule warns us to avoid the construction of a hierarchical order among the observed phenomena. We cannot know at the beginning of our observation which of the phenomena are more or less important.

This is an important warning for therapists. At the beginning certain aspects of a client's situation may stand out, certain symptoms may impress themselves with particular force, certain strands in his or her story catch our imagination and provide us with clues for diagnosis and prognosis. We must, of course, pay attention to these but not at the expense of other aspects which are at this point less telling and distinct.

All three rules are obviously related strands of the same approach – only the context can elucidate a particular situation, and short cuts are likely to land us in a blind alley or lead us to a pseudo-solution. The therapist's task is not easy; what is required could be described – with Freud – as 'free-floating attention'. Openness is needed to avoid premature closure.

ILLUSTRATION

John has been referred to me as 'suffering from a depressive illness' and has been put on antidepressants by a psychiatrist. In many ways he lives up to the image of the depressed client – wearing a dark suit, moving slowly, speaking monotonously, not lifting his eyes from the carpet. In what he says he dwells on things that have gone wrong for him in the past – 'I'm just unable to cope'. The temptation to join my colleague's diagnostic judgement was considerable. However, there were two observations which made me hesitate: he wore red socks, and the top of the Guardian *was peeping out of his carrier bag. The red socks seemed to contradict the monotonous way in which he presented himself. Also, in my experience, severely depressed people are rarely interested in the news of the day.*

These observations do not, of course, show conclusively that John was not depressed – but they helped me to keep myself open for whatever might emerge in future sessions. In fact, John turned out to display a complex oscillation of emotional states and showed himself in the end to be less depressed than confused and emotionally disorientated.

A space for therapy

Most therapists would agree that the space in which therapy takes place contributes to the total therapeutic situation and has, therefore, to be chosen with care. But different therapists will have different views about what this space should be like. One of the main criteria is likely to be the degree of anonymity the therapist considers necessary for the therapeutic process. A readiness for personal disclosure or a stance of neutrality is not only shown by the therapist him or herself but also by the room in which he or she works.

Psychoanalytically oriented therapists tend to prefer an impersonal space; just as they avoid revealing aspects of themselves, they do not wish their working space to do the revealing for them. The need for anonymity is rooted in psychoanalytic theory. As we have seen, transference and the development of a transference neurosis is aided by a screen-like presence of the therapist, which interferes as little as possible with the client's projections. If you see the dismantling of the transference neurosis as an important aspect of therapy, then neutral and impersonal surroundings are desirable. Ideally this means working in a room that is not part of the therapist's living space and does not betray his or her personal taste by the way it is furnished, the books on the shelves (professional books are generally considered to be neutral) or the pictures on the wall. Such an arrangement also leaves the client in ignorance of whether the therapist is married or single and protects him or her from domestic sounds, including those indicating the presence of children.

Even orthodox psychoanalysts do not always adhere to such an 'ideal' model. It is interesting to recall that Freud saw his patients in his own house where he was surrounded by his archaeological collection. One of his analysands, the famous 'wolf-man', commented that he was reminded 'not of a doctor's office but rather of an archaeologist's study' (Gay, 1988: 170). Freud used his statuettes to explain to this patient the similarity between psychoanalysis and archaeology. Freud's own practice broke many of the rules he had laid down for the use of his colleagues: 'He allowed himself cordial comments during the hour. He made friends with his favourite patients', and he conducted some analyses on walks through the streets of Vienna (Gay, 1988: 303). Most psychotherapists, however committed to anonymity, will vary and modify what they may consider the ideal model.

How does the existential therapist choose the 'place for therapy'? She or he does not distinguish between transference and the 'real' therapeutic relationship, as we have seen; the meeting between client and therapist is always a blend of new impressions and anticipations shaped by previous experiences, and this process is mutual. Thus the existential therapist is not concerned with anonymity or impersonality in order to invite the client's phantasy. Nor, from an existential perspective, can a person ever be a screen for the projections of another.

Does this mean that the therapist can behave as he or she would in any other situation? We have already seen that the therapeutic relationship has as its aim the clarification of whatever the client has brought. The therapist's and client's participation in the realization of this aim differ: the client brings narrations, thoughts and feelings describing and arising from his or her situation; the therapist provides the 'space' where these can be seen, clarified and understood. The therapist may also help with the task of clarification by comments and questions but will 'disclose' him or herself only when this might assist the therapeutic aim (Spinelli, 1994: 260 ff.). In any case, the therapist needs to take care not to usurp the client's space. This applies also to the actual space chosen for therapy. It must not be impersonal, for how could a client speak personally in an impersonal space? But if it is cluttered up with the therapist's concerns, problems and involvements, it will inevitably intrude on the space the client needs and has come to use.

Would it perhaps be best if the therapist went to see the client in her or his own home? Apart from the practical difficulties, it could be an intrusion into the client's actual space and may force certain kinds of disclosure the client is not ready to make. The balance between inviting openness and intrusive inhibition is always delicate and can never be easy to find; different therapists may assess it differently. The existential therapist's primary concern is to keep open a therapeutic space for the client.

The couch

It may seem strange to some readers that the use of the couch, a psychoanalytic device *par excellence*, should be discussed at this point. However, it does play a part in the therapeutic approach of some existential therapists. Medard Boss, the creator of 'Daseinsanalysis' and friend of Heidegger, recommends it warmly and at some length.

What were the original reasons for an arrangement where the client lies on a couch while the therapist is sitting out of sight behind his head?

1 Freud admits that it has 'a historical basis' and is 'the remnant of the hypnotic method out of which psycho-analysis was evolved' (1913: 133).
2 Freud adds that he finds it impossible to be 'stared at' for eight hours a day. Also he does not wish to influence his patients by what they may read into his facial expressions.
3 Reclining on the couch is thought to aid 'free association', which in Freud's work had taken the place of hypnosis.
4 It also, in the view of many psychoanalysts, facilitates 'regression'. That is, the return to early traumatic experiences and thus the reworking of unresolved conflicts.

Existential-phenomenologically, I offer the following comments:

1 The existential therapist will avoid 'the residue of the hypnotic treatment', as it perpetuates the imbalance of power which she or he is trying to overcome.
2 Working face-to-face with a client has its difficulties. Both therapist and client should have the freedom to face each other or not, otherwise the meeting can become a trap. This problem can be addressed by putting two chairs at an angle to each other.
3 'Free association' is a misleading term, as chains of associations are expected to lead inevitably to the original conflict. It is a deterministic notion, which was questioned even when Freud first developed the concept. For the existential therapist, whatever is said is the outcome of a present total situation.

4 'Regression' assumes a linear concept of time which is non-existential. We need not 'return' to the past because it is already an aspect of the present, though it may be cut off ('dissociated') from our awareness.

Thus the existential therapist seems to have no reason to put his or her client on the couch. Boss, however, thinks she or he has, and we need to look at what he says about it.

In *Psychoanalysis and Daseinsanalysis* (1963), Boss stresses repeatedly that Freud's practice was in 'intrinsic harmony' with existential ideas, and that a radical difference showed itself only in his theorizing. Thus he recommended the use of the couch, without agreeing with the reasons psychoanalysts give for it. It is questionable whether such a radical split between practice and theory can be made. However, I propose to look at some of the reasons Boss puts forward from an existential point of view, as they raise some issues of general importance.

For to let the patient lie down in the analytic situation takes cognizance of the human body itself as a sphere of human existence; it is not merely an apparatus or an organism attached in some enigmatic way to a psyche. (Boss, 1963: 62)

This is a lucid and precise analysis of how existential phenomenologists see the relation between body and mind, but I fail to see why lying down should imply a greater acknowledgement of the body 'as a sphere of human existence' than sitting up.

The conventional arrangement in which physician and patient sit facing each other corresponds – as far as the respective bodily sphere of their existence is concerned – to the traditional conception of two subjects, separate and standing opposite each other. (Boss, 1963: 62–3)

It seems to me that physician and patient are even more separate when one is lying down and the other is sitting up.

Erect stature is the position *par excellence* of self-assertion. It accentuates self-glorification, as much as the supremacy of everything that belongs to the head. (Boss, 1963: 63)

If this is so, would it not equally apply to the therapist who should then be lying down too?

> Freud himself has pointed out that the mere visual perception of the concrete presence of the therapist who sits opposite the patient insurmountably obstructs the rise of all possibilities of behaving which are too infantile, and are therefore repulsed. Actually, the situation then appears to be a dialogue between two equally grown-up partners. This means that the position of the partners' bodily realms of existence in no way corresponds to the child-like nature of much of the patients' being, which is especially in need of psychotherapy. (Boss, 1963: 63–4)

It seems to me that at this point psychoanalytic practice has pushed aside existential theory. What Boss is talking about here sounds very much like lying down as a form of regression so that more infantile layers can be reached – a psychoanalytic rather than an existential notion.

Interpretation

When discussing the therapist's contribution to the clarification of whatever the client brings we have mentioned comments and questions. Does this mean that the therapist 'interprets' what the client says, and has such an interpretation a place in existential psychotherapy?

First of all, it is important to see that all perception is inevitably interpretational (cf. Spinelli, 1989). Each of us will experience the world from the particular and unique position in which our experiential, relational and sociocultural situation has placed us. None of us can be simply a mirror which reflects the world. All perception is interpretation. But we need to distinguish between different kinds of interpretation. The two interpretational modes likely to be used by the therapist are either 'reductive' or 'hermeneutic'.

Hermeneutics is 'the method of interpretation first of texts, and secondly of the whole social, historical and psychological world' (Blackburn, 1994: 172). (Hermes, in Greek mythology, is the messenger of the gods and the carrier of communication.) The increasing concern of hermeneutics with meaning and under-standing found one of its most important protagonists in the philosopher Wilhelm Dilthey (1833-1911), often seen as a precursor of the phenomenologists, who stressed the inevitable incompleteness of all understanding. Interpretation as used in psychoanalysis is more restricted. Walrond-Skinner defines it as 'a communication from therapist to patient designed to elucidate the unconscious meaning and repressed wishes which lie beneath his dreams, free associations, use of symbolism and/or feelings towards the therapist expressed through the transference' (1986: 188). The essential feature of this kind of interpretation is that the experience itself, the phenomenon, is reduced to something else – to 'trends which are only hypothetical', to use Freud's words (1916: 67 [1: 95]). Here the 'real' (unconscious) meaning underneath the (conscious) phenomenon is hidden from the client but can be deciphered by the therapist. An existential-phenomenological approach, on the other hand, will try to discover the fuller meaning of the phenomenon, be it a symbol, a symptom or a dream. The fuller meaning may at first sight be hidden from both client and therapist, but can be 'unfolded', to use Ricoeur's striking expression (Ricoeur, 1974: 13), by common exploration.

A reductive interpretation tends to lose the original experience, whereas in the hermeneutic interpretation the original experience (the phenomenon) remains at the core of the interpretation. Analytically a snake disappears behind the phallus; hermeneutically it stays at the centre of the interpretation displaying the full range of its manifold meanings.

ILLUSTRATION

Mary arrives for her session in a state of great agitation. She has left her handbag on the train. This has never happened to her before, and she is shocked.

Most psychoanalysts would interpret the handbag as a symbol of femininity, many would quite concretely regard it as a symbol of the womb. Its loss would mean a kind of female equivalent of castration, and leaving it on the train might indicate that Mary either feels she has lost her femininity or is afraid she may do so, or even wishes to get rid of it. An exploration of her sexual situation (Has she a sexual partner? Is she near the menopause? Does she fear a hysterectomy?) would clarify the meaning of her loss.

Existential-phenomenologically the primary meaning of a handbag can only be that of a handbag. If it has any additional meaning, we cannot know this unless the client tells us so. It would, of course, have been quite possible for Mary to say something like, 'without my handbag I feel less like a woman' – but she did not. Like any thing or person in this world, a handbag is part of a wider context. It is this context which the existential therapist tries to explore.

I asked Mary what this handbag meant to her, but this did not seem to lead anywhere. I then turned to her great agitation and wondered what she felt without her handbag. Her answer was emphatic: 'Naked! I don't really mind losing this handbag, it is the credit cards I mind and the card from the library and also some letters – I know it sounds silly but it feels as if I could no longer show who I am.'

There are, of course, many reasons why we might leave something on the train, and there is also such a thing as absent-mindedness. But it may be important to look at our response to such a loss. It was the desperate quality of Mary's agitation which led us to the understanding that Mary was defending herself against overwhelming feelings of insecurity ('I could no longer show who I am') by expressing such extreme concern for her lost handbag.

References

Blackburn, S. (1994) *Oxford Dictionary of Philosophy*. Oxford: Oxford University Press.

Boss, M. (1963) *Psychoanalysis and Daseinsanalysis*. New York: Basic Books.

Freud, S. (1910) *The Future Prospects of Psycho-Analytic Therapy*. S.E. XI. London: Hogarth Press.

Freud, S. (1913) *On Beginning the Treatment*. S.E. XII. London: Hogarth Press.

Freud, S. (1915) *Observations on Transference-Love*. S.E. XII. London: Hogarth Press.

Freud, S. (1916) *Introductory Lectures on Psycho-Analysis*. S.E. XV. London: Hogarth Press. (Pelican Freud Library. Vol. 1. Harmondsworth: Penguin Books.)

Freud, S. (1917) *Introductory Lectures on Psycho-Analysis*. S.E. XVI. London: Hogarth Press. (Pelican Freud Library. Vol. 1. Harmondsworth: Penguin Books.)

Gay, P. (1988) *Freud. A Life for our Time*. London: Dent.

Heimann, P. (1989) *About Children and Children-No-Longer. Collected Papers 1942–1980*. London: Tavistock-Routledge.

Hinshelwood, R.D. (1989) *A Dictionary of Kleinian Thought*. London: Free Association Books.

Moore, B.E. and Fine, B.D. (1990) *Psychoanalytic Terms and Concepts*. New Haven: American Psychoanalytic Association.
Ricoeur, P. (1974) *The Conflict of Interpretations*. Evanston: Northwestern University Press.
Spinelli, E. (1989) *The Interpreted World. An Introduction to Phenomenological Psychology*. London: Sage.
Spinelli, E. (1994) *Demystifying Therapy*. London: Constable.
Walrond-Skinner, S. (1986) *Dictionary of Psychotherapy*. London: Routledge & Kegan Paul.

5

Existential-phenomenological Dimensions of Groups

We can understand the process of individuals relating to each other in two different ways. We can either see them as essentially separate entities between whom a relation can but need not be established, or we can see them as always and inevitably in a context with others.

As 'relationship' implies something to be achieved or lacking, something that can be good or bad, it might be better to talk of 'relatedness', a word that is judgementally neutral. If we take relatedness as our starting point, if we see individuals always in a context with others, then withdrawal from relationship or the denial of its importance are particular forms of relatedness. Relatedness then seems to be an aspect of existence itself, what Heidegger calls an 'existential' – a 'given' – to which we can respond in different ways.

Conceiving of individuals as separate entities reflects Descartes's separation of the individual mind as a 'thinking non-extended thing' (Cottingham, 1993: 124) from the rest of the world. The unextended, that is the bodiless, mind has to cross a gap in order to reach other minds who are part of a world whose very existence we cannot take for granted. The psychoanalytic approach is an attempt to cross this gap, and its concepts of projection, introjection and identification are ingenuous constructions to explain the interaction of individuals across a divide. In contrast the existential-phenomenological approach sees relatedness as an aspect of existence. Being is always 'Being-with-others' (Heidegger, 1962: 155), the world is a 'with-world'. We are always in a relational field, in a state of intersubjectivity. There is no gap to be bridged.

Our definition of groups will depend on our point of departure. If individuals are essentially separate entities, a group is the result

of a number of people coming together in order to do something –
the formation of a group has to be negotiated. But if individuals
are always in a context with others, if being a member of a group
is an aspect of 'Being-in-the-world', we need to decide how to
respond to this. More specifically, we need to decide what shape
we wish to give to this existential fact of group relatedness by
joining and creating particular forms of group relationship, be it
by joining a therapeutic group or creating a family. We can, of
course, also choose to avoid groups.

Three types of therapeutic groups

It is customary to distinguish three types of group therapy:
therapy *in* the group, therapy *with* the group and therapy *of* the
group. These types of group therapy each have their representatives.

The therapist works with an individual in the group   This is
individual therapy in a group setting where the extent of the
group members' contribution varies. An example of this is the
therapist's work with a client 'in the hot seat' in a gestalt group.
But the situation can arise temporarily in all kinds of groups.

*The therapist works with the whole group as if it were an indi-
vidual*   This is essentially a psychoanalytic approach and is most
strikingly illustrated by the work of W.R. Bion. We shall address
ourselves to his method at a later stage when we compare it with
that of S.H. Foulkes. At this point it needs only to be said that in
such a group the therapist's main concern is with lifting into the
consciousness of group members those impulses and desires
which derive from an unconscious shared by the group – a
process not very different from that at work in an individual
psychoanalytic session.

The group is the therapist of the group   Here the group members
themselves play a central part in the therapeutic process. The
therapist will tend slowly to move into the periphery of group
events. Change comes about through communication and
interaction. This is the model of Foulkes and it comes nearest to
an existential-phenomenological approach to groups; we shall
concern ourselves with it at greater length below.

The approach of W.R. Bion

After studying history and medicine, Bion trained as a psychoanalyst and was analysed by Melanie Klein, whose ideas he adopted and elaborated. Though his interest in groups was comparatively short-lived, his influence on group theory was considerable. Bion's concepts did not only find their way into group therapy but also into the understanding of organizations and therapeutic communities (Hinshelwood, 1989: 229).

Bion's approach to group therapy is essentially psychoanalytic. Even a brief survey shows it to be markedly unphenomenological, putting emphasis on unobservable psychic processes with little concern for the actual communication between group members.

Bion sees the group as a number of people coming together to fulfil a certain task which is consciously defined. But the group aims are sabotaged by the emergence of three basic assumptions which need to be acknowledged for the 'work' to be accomplished. These assumptions emerge from 'a pool to which anonymous contributions are made, and through which the impulses and desires implicit in these contributions are gratified' (Bion, 1961: 50). These basic assumptions are:

(a) *dependency* on the leader which leads to idealization and disappointment;
(b) *fight* against or *flight* from an imaginary 'enemy' whereby the leader is expected to play the part of the decisive authority;
(c) the *pairing* of two group members of whatever gender in a discussion while the others sit in silence – a discussion which is experienced by the group as a messianic symbol of the birth of new ideas and a new leader.

It is the therapist's task to interpret these assumptions and, since they involve him or her, these interpretations are essentially transferential. The group is seen as if it were one patient, where the unconscious is shared by all group members – a common 'pool' – and thus the emerging impulses are presumed to be shared by everyone. The interaction between group members is seen as unconscious, an interaction of needs, defences and anxieties. There is no relational field and the conscious interplay is not addressed.

The striking characteristics of Bion's view are his disregard of the individual voice and the neglect of his own position in the group. While he sees himself as a receiver of 'projections' Bion ignores the powerful influence of the therapist on what occurs. We will see that Foulkes's approach went in a different direction altogether, and one which is nearer to an existential-phenomenological view.

The approach of S.H. Foulkes

Foulkes (1898–1976) was trained as a psychoanalyst in Vienna, but there were other important influences in his professional life which took him beyond psychoanalysis and even into opposition to some of its tenets.

First, though Foulkes frequently denied the influence of Kurt Lewin's group dynamic concepts, at least in one place he did admit to a common view: 'For our orientation to the hospital "therapeutic community" at Northfield, we found that our own group-analytic views married well with concepts used in "field theory", and that the latter helped us in our orientation. Here belongs, for instance, the concept of a social field' (Foulkes and Anthony, 1965: 20). Lewin's 'field theory' proposes that each individual exists in a psychological field of forces that determines his or her behaviour, and he calls this 'the life space'. The emphasis here is on the total situation, on interaction rather than the coexistence of self-sufficient entities. We are reminded of Merleau-Ponty's concern with intersubjectivity and Heidegger's 'with-world'. We also find an echo of this view in Foulkes's concept of 'matrix': 'the common shared ground which ultimately determines the meaning and significance of all events and upon which all communications and interpretations, verbal and non-verbal, rest' (Foulkes, 1964: 292).

Secondly, admitting the relevance of Lewin's 'field theory' to his own approach, Foulkes added: 'Further, there is a common background as regards Gestalt psychology' (Foulkes and Anthony, 1965: 20). Lewin's contact with gestalt psychology was at the Berlin Psychological Institute where he worked at the same time as the gestalt psychologists Wertheimer and Köhler. Foulkes, on the other hand, attended lectures of the gestalt psychologist

Adhemar Gelb at the Frankfurt Neurological Institute. The crucial aspect of this 'common background' was the belief in context, the proposition that 'the whole was more than the sum of its parts', which is reflected in both Lewin's 'field' and Foulkes's 'matrix'. Thirdly at the Frankfurt Neurological Institute Foulkes also met the biologist Kurt Goldstein, whose influence he gladly acknowledged. Goldstein blended ideas rooted in gestalt psychology with phenomenological notions. He was interested in philosophy and familiar with some of the ideas of Husserl, Heidegger and Merleau-Ponty. Spiegelberg discusses Goldstein's contribution to phenomenology and presents the gist of it in the following way:

(a) All phenomena need to be recorded with an open mind.
(b) 'The premature straight-jacketing of the phenomena by pre-conceived theories' (Spiegelberg, 1972: 308) is to be avoided.
(c) Each phenomenon 'needs to be seen in relation to the organism and the situation in which it appears' (Spiegelberg, 1972: 308).

It is through Goldstein's teaching that phenomenological ideas entered Foulkes' thinking. Though Foulkes never referred to his approach as phenomenological, he was very eloquent in stressing the effect Goldstein's ideas had on his own concepts. Talking about his introduction of the term 'network' into his theory of groups, Foulkes said:

The term *network* was used to express the fact that our individual patient is, in essence, merely a symptom of a disturbance of equilibrium in the intimate network of which he is a part. Personally I used the term *network* deliberately in analogy to my teacher in the mid-twenties, the neurobiologist Kurt Goldstein, then in Frankfurt. He was a pioneer of the view that the nervous system can best be understood in theory and practice not as a complicated sum of individual neurons but that on the contrary it reacts consistently as a whole. He called this a network and called the individual neuron cell a *nodal point*. For this reason I called the total system of persons who belong together in their reaction a network, and the *individuals* composing it correspond to *nodal points*. (Foulkes, 1975: 12)

That the individual is always part of a network is the idea which pervades the whole of Foulkes's thinking about groups.

The priority of the group

Even in his first book Foulkes was expressing most emphatically his belief in the importance of the total human situation, in which the individual is first of all the member of a group: 'Each individual – itself an artificial, though plausible abstraction – is basically and centrally determined, inevitably, by the world in which he lives, by the community, the group, of which he forms a part' (Foulkes, 1948: 10). This essentially non-Cartesian stance he elaborated on a later occasion:

In recent times, in fact since the end of the Renaissance . . . a configuration has arisen that has brought about the idea of the individual existing in isolation. The individual is then confronted with the community and the world as if they were outside of him. The philosophy of Descartes starts from this premise, and its strict subject/object juxtaposition is still responsible for many pseudo problems of our time. (Foulkes, 1990: 152)

In his concern with context, with the priority of the group, the 'openness' of the individual to a constant interaction with the world, Foulkes expressed a view which was in many ways non-psychoanalytical. In fact, he criticized the psychoanalytic approach at times quite specifically: 'What is inside is outside, the "social" is not external but very much internal too and penetrates the innermost being of the individual personality'. Foulkes continues, in the same passage: 'the psychoanalytic point of view should be seen as a deliberate abstraction, the individual being deliberately abstracted and considered isolated from his context' (1990: 227).

When commenting on a paper by Fairbairn, Foulkes refers to 'Freud's concepts of ego, id and superego' as 'constructions abstracted from the living organism which must be perceived as a whole in action' (1990: 113). This is a critique of psychoanalytic concepts from a phenomenological point of view – though Foulkes never said so. It is important to note that Foulkes distinguished group analysis from psychoanalysis. It was the group and not a psyche that was being analysed: 'Both aspects, the individual and the social one, are not only integrated in our approach, but their artificial isolation – never found in actual reality – does not arise' (Foulkes, 1990: 148).

The Frankfurt Psychoanalytic Institute, of which Foulkes was a member, shared a house with the Institut für Sozialforschung, which later became known as the Frankfurt School. The two institutes exchanged ideas and held joint seminars. The Frankfurt School had integrated some of the ideas of the German philosopher Wilhelm Dilthey, who is often seen as a precursor of the phenomenological orientation. Dilthey knew Husserl, who is said to have been impressed by Dilthey. Once again phenomenological ideas were in the air – as they had been with Kurt Goldstein – without being acknowledged as such by Foulkes. However, Foulkes would not have denied that the sociological dimension of his thinking was influenced by this early background which combined psychoanalytic with sociological notions.

The importance of communication

Foulkes saw psychological disturbance as essentially a disturbance of communication, a kind of extreme individualism that rejects contact with others. The neurotic position is 'in its very nature highly individualistic. It is group disruptive in essence, for it is genetically the result of an incompatibility between the individual and his original group' (Foulkes, 1964: 89). The healing process is therefore the creation of new lines of communication: 'Working towards an ever more articulate form of communication is identical to the therapeutic process itself' (Foulkes, 1948: 169).

The important point here is that therapy is not seen as a rebalancing of an internal psychic structure but as a process that takes place in the area *between* people. Thus the group is seen by Foulkes as the therapeutic field *par excellence*.

The concept of the mind

Foulkes's definition of mind is another aspect of his 'philosophy' (an expression he used in one of his late papers), which shows strong affinities with a phenomenological approach:

'I do not think that the mind is basically inside the person as an individual . . . The mind that is usually called intrapsychic is a property of the group, and the processes that take place are due to the dynamic interactions in this communicational matrix. Correspondingly we cannot make the conventional sharp differentiation between inside and outside, or between phantasy and reality. (Foulkes, 1990: 277-8)

In his very last paper, which was published after his death, Foulkes put it more succinctly:

What is called 'the mind' consists of interacting processes between a number of closely linked persons, commonly called a group. . . . This totally new phenomenon which they create I usually refer to as the 'context of the group'. I do not talk of a group mind because this is a substantivation of what is meant and as unsatisfactory as speaking of an individual mind. The mind is not a *thing* which exists but a series of events moving and proceeding all the time. (1990: 224)

It is tempting to say that these are ideas which Foulkes expressed only in papers at the end of his life, and it is true that he had not elaborated them to this extent before. It is striking that they are absent in his last textbook, *Group-Analytic Psychotherapy. Method and Principles*, which appeared shortly before his death. But it is also important to remember that his first book, published thirty years earlier, contained the following: 'Progress in all the sciences during the last decades has led to the same independent and concerted conclusion: that the old juxtaposition of an inside and outside world, constitution and environment, individual and society, phantasy and reality, body and mind and so on, are untenable' (Foulkes, 1948: 10).

This phenomenological dimension of Foulkes's thinking, anti-Cartesian in its rejection of the division between mind and world, is interspersed with psychoanalytic notions as we will see when we examine the special characteristics of group analysis as seen by Foulkes.

The special characteristics of group analysis

In *Group Psychotherapy. The Psychoanalytic Approach* (first published in 1957), written by Foulkes together with E.J. Anthony, we find a chapter called 'The Phenomenology of the Group Situation' – a summary of group phenomena which shows a mixture of phenomenological and psychoanalytic notions:

1   *Socialization through the group* makes it possible for the individual group member to break through his or her isolation and participate in a process of intercommunication: 'references to "I" and "me" alter to "we" and "us"' (Foulkes and Anthony, 1965: 149).

2   *The 'mirror' phenomena*   Here the 'individual is confronted with various aspects of his social, psychological, or body image' (Foulkes and Anthony, 1965: 150). The group member discovers that his or her identity is established *between* him or herself and others.

3   *The 'chain' phenomena* concept takes the place of 'free association'. This is 'free-floating discussion' and occurs when each member contributes his or her 'link' to the group theme. This process of communication has none of the more mechanistic aspects of the original concept of free association.

4   *Theorizing* is inevitable in the early stages of group work. Each member has his or her own 'theories' about the 'causes' of their condition. It is not the therapist's task to 'correct' the members' 'fiction' but to enable them to reach a clearer understanding through intercommunication.

5   *Support* by the group for each group member is essentially therapeutic: the group takes over the therapist's task of understanding and clarifying the individual client's attempts to come to terms with his or her conflicts by its attitude of 'letting be'.

6   *Silences* 'represent an important communication in the group and the therapist must endeavour to understand the many different meanings' (Foulkes and Anthony, 1965: 156).

7   *The 'condenser' phenomenon* is 'the sudden discharge of deep and primitive material following the pooling of associated ideas in the group' (Foulkes and Anthony, 1965: 151). This discharge takes the form of fears and phantasies. The authors compare it with the emergence of Bion's basic assumptions, and the process described is clearly psychoanalytic.

8   *Resonance* is not seen as an inevitable intersubjective phenomenon but as a 'fixated' or 'regressed' member's response to a

group event which touches the level of psycho-social development at which she or he is 'set' (Foulkes and Anthony, 1965: 152).

9 *Scapegoating* This process is understood psychoanalytically as the group's 'urgent need . . . to punish' which 'meets an urgent need in a particular member to be punished' (Foulkes and Anthony, 1965: 157).

These group phenomena are presented in the Foulkes and Anthony text in a different order. My order of presentation aims to emphasize the two different approaches used: points 7–9 are clearly based on psychoanalytic notions, while 1–6 show a phenomenological dimension. *Group Psychotherapy*, as mentioned above, has two authors – Foulkes and Anthony. The chapter from which I have taken the characteristics of group phenomena was written by Anthony, but we have no reason to assume that the two authors did not agree.

It was noted above that Foulkes makes a clear distinction between psychoanalysis and group analysis. What emerges from this comparison is that Foulkes did not see group analysis as an applied psychoanalysis. The group situation is 'multipersonal' and does not encourage regression or a regressive transference relationship with the therapist. While the position of the analyst is characterized as one of 'relative anonymity and passivity' in the case of psychoanalysis, the analyst's role in the group, as described by Foulkes, is 'relatively realistic' and shows 'interaction with others'. There is in group analysis 'an emphasis on reaction and experience in the present situation ("here-and-now"), and the group-analytic experience is "corrective" – "ego training in action"' (Foulkes and Anthony, 1965: 52).

Though Foulkes clearly emphasizes the distinction between psychoanalysis and group analysis, he does not here criticize psychoanalytic concepts as such. But it would not be true to say that such criticism appeared only in his later writings. At the same time as *Group Psychotherapy* appeared, Foulkes published a comment on a paper by Fairbairn (referred to earlier) in which he says: 'The basic objection remains that in psychoanalysis physical concepts are being applied, either directly or via biology, to a medium for which they are inadequate, that of human interaction, i.e. psychology' (Foulkes, 1990: 109).

There can be no doubt that Foulkes's attitude towards the psychoanalytic approach remained ambivalent. There are basic objections to be found throughout his writings, and his critique seems essentially phenomenologically informed but – like so many theorists and practitioners rooted in the original psycho-analytic project – he could never completely break away from this background.

Towards an existential-phenomenological approach to group therapy

Currently there exists no detailed existential-phenomenological approach to group therapy. The following list suggests a skeleton structure for such an approach.

1   If 'Being-in-the-world' always means 'Being-with-others', if the world is essentially a 'with-world' – a relational field – then the 'individual' is indeed an 'abstraction', as Foulkes says, and can only be understood in a context of mutual disclosure.
2   What we see as psychological disturbances are then disturb-ances in this context, disturbances of relatedness and com-munication.
3   The therapeutic group provides a context in which these relational and communicative disturbances can be observed *in situ*, so to speak. Relational and communicative failure can be experienced, and the possibilities of different ways of relating and communicating can be explored.
4   The group therapist is a member of the group with a specific task – to assist in the process of clarifying the relational and communicative disturbances and potentialities of the group. It is important that she or he does not see her or himself as being 'outside' and 'above' the group. Heidegger's definition of 'others' is relevant here: 'By "others" we do not mean every-one else but me – those over against the "I" stands out. They are rather those from whom, for the most part, one does *not* distinguish oneself – those among whom one is too' (Heidegger, 1962: 154). In an existential-phenomenological group, the therapist does not 'stand out' hierarchically 'over against' the others.

5 Interpretations of group events are essentially the task of group members. They are not a reduction of these events to other (earlier) occurrences, though remembering those may enrich and clarify what is experienced in the group now. Group phenomena have, of course, past roots and future possibilities - but these are inevitably part of the present experience. The group therapist's principal task is to keep the group space open for such interpretations to be made.

6 The reliving of past relationships in the present group situation - what psychoanalysts call 'transference' - is not primarily focused on the therapist but dispersed among members within the group. It is an example of the multidimensionality of time, and needs of course to be understood and clarified. Again, the therapist's task is that of an enabler rather than the principal interpreter.

7 There is no reason why the therapist should not contribute his or her own understanding and feelings to the group process. The question that will arise is the same that arises whenever the therapist chooses a form of 'self disclosure' as means of intervention: who is it she or he is trying to help - the client(s), or her or himself?

   Another question arises with any form of helping intervention. Heidegger distinguishes between two kinds of 'solicitude' - 'that which leaps in and dominates, and that which leaps forth and liberates' (1962: 159). Heidegger is not talking about therapeutic help but the distinction seems relevant to a consideration of the therapist's task. Leaping 'in', supporting the client 'in order to take away his "care"' tends to create dependency. In existential group work the therapist's task is to help the client to meet his or her difficulties, 'to give [them] back . . . authentically as such for the first time' (1962: 159).

8 Some group therapeutic approaches stress the necessity to focus on what happens 'within' the group and ignore what members bring into it from 'outside'. We have already seen that Foulkes thought that such a dichotomy was untenable and that the 'outside' always penetrated the 'inside'. In an existential-phenomenological approach, with its emphasis on context, the possibility of such a division does not arise. Whatever group members talk about is talked about *in* the group and is thus relevant to it.

This sketchy outline of some of the thinking which would form the theoretical framework for existential-phenomenological groupwork contains a number of ideas expressed by Foulkes, who – in spite of some psychoanalytical residues – came nearest to creating a phenomenological theory of groups. Unfortunately existential thinkers and therapists have not yet concerned themselves, in any detail, with group phenomena.

References

Bion, W.R. (1961) *Experiences in Groups and Other Papers*. London: Tavistock/Routledge.

Cottingham, J. (1993) *A Descartes Dictionary*. Oxford: Blackwell.

Foulkes, S.H. (1948) *Introduction to Group-Analytic Psychotherapy. Studies in the Social Integration of Individuals and Groups*. London: Karnac Books.

Foulkes, S.H. (1964) *Therapeutic Group Analysis*. London: Karnac Books.

Foulkes, S.H. (1975) *Group-Analytic Psychotherapy. Method and Principles*. London: Karnac Books.

Foulkes, S.H. (1990) *Selected Papers*. Ed. Elizabeth Foulkes. London: Karnac Books.

Foulkes, S.H. and Anthony, E.J. (1965) *Group Psychotherapy. The Psychoanalytic Approach*. 2nd edn. London: Karnac Books.

Heidegger, M. (1962) *Being and Time*. Tr. J. Macquarrie and E. Robinson. London: Blackwell.

Hinshelwood, R.D. (1989) *A Dictionary of Kleinian Thought*. London: Free Association Books.

Spiegelberg, H. (1972) *Phenomenology in Psychology and Psychiatry: A Historical Introduction*. Evanston: Northwestern University Press.

6

Mind and Body

Descartes and the mind–body split

Questions about the nature of mind and body, and their relation to each other, have preoccupied our thinking in different ways throughout our history. Western thinking has been inclined to see them as separate entities and then found itself face to face with the puzzle of their interaction. Even before Descartes's radical dualism, the Augustinian-Platonic tradition ascribed all 'higher' psychological functions to the 'soul' in a world apart from 'matter', that is from the body. It is worth while returning to Descartes's own writings to contact the depth of the division he made between body and mind: 'This "I" – that is the soul by which I am what I am – is entirely distinct from the body, and would not fail to be whatever it is even if the body did not exist' (Cottingham, 1993: 54). We see that for Descartes the 'mind' is 'res cogitans' (the thinking substance) and the body is 'res extensa' (the extended substance) which is part of the material world. Descartes did not deny the fact of interaction between mind and body but did not seem clear about the manner in which it could take place. At one point he suggested that the pineal gland in the brain was the location for such an interaction.

Once you have separated mind from body and see them as two distinct entities, it is in fact very difficult to explain their interaction. Leibniz's proposition of a 'pre-established harmony' assumes that God guarantees a non-causal correspondence between them – there is no interaction but a 'psycho-physical parallelism' as it was later called.

Though dualistic thinking seems to influence the imagination of most people, there are also monistic theories which deny the reality of a second substance, be it body or mind. Materialism sees the mind as an 'epiphenomenon' (that is an incidental product which is powerless in itself) of the body, while idealism denies reality to anything but the mind. For a monistic approach the problem of interaction does not arise.

Descartes's view on science

Descartes is often seen not only as the founding father of modern philosophy but also the theorist of modern science. His views on what science should be certainly had an important impact on later conceptions of its nature. He saw the material world – and that included the body, as we have seen – as a 'machine' obeying the laws of Newtonian physics, and this led to an explanatory framework which was essentially mechanistic. So he could say: 'It is no less natural for a clock constructed with this or that set of wheels to tell the time than it is for a tree which grew from this or that seed to produce the appropriate fruit' (Cottingham, 1993: 111).

Descartes had the vision of a 'general' science where the approach to knowledge was independent of what the object of this knowledge was. Thus the various disciplines have a common ground as 'they consider nothing but the various proportions or relations between their objects' (Cottingham, 1993: 100).

When psychoanalysis presented itself as a science, it seems to have aspired to the Cartesian model in its attempts to reduce a multitude of phenomena to a small number of basic principles. This is demonstrated in its preference for mechanistic explanations and spatial metaphors. (Descartes's comparison of a tree bearing fruit with a clock reminds us of Freud's image of the mind as a 'psychical apparatus'.)

Freud and the psychosomatic problem

Freud's views on the relation between body and mind have been presented with great erudition in two important papers by David L. Smith. He describes how Freud moved from a Cartesian dualism to a materialistic monism which sees 'the mental [as] a property of some neural processes' (Smith, 1992: 155). He quotes a sentence from the opening paragraph of Freud's early work *Project for a Scientific Psychology* which defines Freud's position very clearly: 'The intention is to furnish a psychology that shall be a natural science: that is, to represent psychical processes as quantitatively determinate states of specifiable material particles' (Freud, 1950: 295). In a later paper Smith emphasizes that 'Freud retained his allegiance to the identity theory, to materialism, for the rest of his life' (Smith, 1995: 396). The identity theory of mind proposes the identity of brain and mind and thus is clearly opposed to Descartes's distinction between mind and body.

But though Freud may have retained his allegiance to the identity theory throughout his life, he seems at times to betray more dualistic tendencies. He wrote, for instance, in *On Narcissism*: 'we must recollect that all our provisional ideas in psychology will presumably some day be based on an organic substructure' (Freud, 1914: 78 [11: 71]). Here Freud seems less certain of monism but 'presumes' that it is likely to be demonstrated by some future discovery. In two other places, an altogether more dualistic note is sounded. In *Notes upon a Case of Obsessional Neurosis* he speaks of 'the leap from a mental process to a somatic innervation – hysterical conversion – which can never be fully comprehensible to us' (Freud, 1909: 157 [9: 38]). In his *Introductory Lectures on Psycho-Analysis* he again refers to 'the puzzling leap from the mental to the physical' (Freud, 1917: 258 [1: 297]). This leap conjures up the old Cartesian gap. Psychoanalytic approaches have, in my view, left this gap unclosed. The interaction between subject and world remains as difficult to explain for psychoanalysis as for Descartes – after all, projections, introjections and identifications are all 'leaps', and a *leap* is not a *link*.

'Psychosomatic conditions', a psychoanalytic dictionary tells us, are 'medical entities in which psychological factors are thought to play a special role in the etiology . . . of the disease' (Moore and Fine, 1990: 157). 'Aetiology' is defined in the *Concise Oxford Dictionary* as 'the science of the causes of disease'. But Freud, the neurologist, clearly did not altogether believe in 'psychological factors' as the 'cause' of physical manifestations – otherwise he would not have spoken of a 'puzzling leap' from the mental to the physical which would 'never be fully comprehensible to us'.

The existential-phenomenological approach

The separation of mind from body is in fact an intellectual speculation, not a reflection on our actual experience. Human existence
is 'embodied'. In Boss's words: 'man's somatic aspect is inseparable from his being-in-the-world. Man also participates bodily in
all his world-relations. Corporality belongs so immediately to
man's existence that we always *are* the corporality also' (Boss,
1963: 142). Merleau-Ponty stresses the embodiment of all perception and interaction: 'It is through my body that I understand
other people, just as it is through my body that I perceive
"things"' (Merleau-Ponty, 1962: 186).

The separation of mind from body was one result of Descartes's
radical scepticism. This scepticism made him doubt the reality of
everything except the doubting (that is 'thinking') and the
disembodied mind. It is this split that needed healing before the
mind–body dichotomy could disappear. The healing move was
made by Edward Husserl who, developing an idea of his teacher
Franz Brentano, pointed out the incompleteness of Descartes's
famous 'I think, therefore I am'. Thinking as such, Husserl
maintained, was impossible. Thinking is always thinking *something*, is directed towards something, is intentional. The isolation
of a thinking mind is untenable. Mind and world are not apart –
the mind 'thinks' world, and to the extent to which Descartes had
seen the body as part of the world, mind and body are not
separate.

Heidegger expresses this mutual involvement of mind and
world as 'Being-in-the-world' which is also a Being-in-the-body. It
is this 'double-aspect' of existence as mind *and* world that
underlies Merleau-Ponty's concept of the human being as an
'incarnate subject' (1962: 185).

This relation between mind and body is not seen as *causal*.
Mental and bodily aspects of existence are always involved
simultaneously, though sometimes one aspect and sometimes the
other is accentuated: 'Man taken as a concrete being is not a
psyche joined to an organism, but the movement to and fro of
existence which at one time allows itself to take corporeal form
and at others moves towards personal acts' (Merleau-Ponty, 1962:
88). This echoes a voice from the distant past, the voice of
Spinoza: 'Mind and body are one and the same individual which is

conceived now under the attribute of thought, and now under the attribute of extension' (1985: 467).

Clinical relevance

From the existential-phenomenological viewpoint, the psychosomatic symptom is not the consequence of a repressed emotion or conflict, that is, not the *effect* of a *cause*. This also implies that one is not prior to the other. Rather it is the disturbance of a total situation, truly 'psychosomatic' as both psyche and soma are simultaneously affected. No 'leap' needs to be made as no gap has to be bridged. The following are examples which will illustrate this:

(a) *Blushing* We do not blush *because* we are ashamed. Instead, there is a total situation we call 'being ashamed', in which both our body (through the widening of the blood vessels underneath the skin) and a complex web of emotions (which we call 'feeling ashamed') *simultaneously* participate.

(b) *Anxiety* Palpitations, sweaty hands and giddiness are not *caused* by anxiety. They are part of a total anxious state which manifests itself both physically and, at the same time, as a characteristic feeling – Heidegger called it mood or attunement – we have come to call 'anxiety'.

(c) *Peptic ulcer* Psychoanalytically, gastric hypersecretion leading to ulceration of the stomach wall is seen as *due* to an unacknowledged hunger for oral care resulting in a state of dependency. An existential-phenomenological approach would perceive it as a total situation of longing to be cared for, which manifests itself both physically *and* emotionally as a feeling of frustration and emptiness. Again there is no causal link between the disturbances of stomach and emotional balance, rather both mind and body participate in the experience of a vacuum that cries out to be filled.

ILLUSTRATION 1

George is a pilot. For some time he has been developing symptoms that trouble him: his heart is beating fast, his pulse is irregular and his palms are sweating.

Medical examination finds no physical reasons for these disturbances which appear suddenly at frequent intervals. When he was a teenager, he tells me, he was afraid of flying but determined to overcome his fear. 'When I started training to be a pilot, my fear disappeared completely.'

Psychodynamically we could say that he had repressed his original anxiety which now returns converted into the physical symptoms of anxiety.

Phenomenologically we see these symptoms as part of a wider state of anxiety, affecting both his emotional and somatic being, and that his 'dissociation' from it has been more successful in the emotional than in the physical realm. It was the task of the therapy to help him to face the anxiety he had originally disowned and explore it. In fact it took some time before he could experience the anxiety accompanying his attacks. This anxiety was an all-pervading feeling of being at risk.

ILLUSTRATION 2

Jean is a desperate person who finds life an intolerable burden. She frequently suffers from severe flu-like illnesses which force her to go to bed. During these times, however, she is surprisingly light-hearted and even humorous.

It would be difficult to understand this cyclical happening in terms of regression and conversion. It appears as if her despair moves from the emotional aspect of her being to the somatic and back again – almost as if a heavy parcel is moved from one hand to the other. This seems like an illustration of Merleau-Ponty's 'movement to and fro of existence which at one time allows itself to take corporeal form and at others moves towards personal acts' (1962: 88).

ILLUSTRATION 3

Tom, a university student suffering from eczema, had been sent to me by his general practitioner. The eczema particularly affected his hands and neck and had been troubling him since childhood. In many children eczema disappears when they grow up, but Tom's persisted after a break of a few years. Medical help had proved unsuccessful. Certain types of eczema have long been considered to show emotional aspects, and it is not surprising that Tom was referred by his doctor to a psychotherapist.

Our attempts to connect Tom's sporadic attacks with specific stressful events were on the whole unsuccessful. He seemed a tense and withdrawn young man who appeared almost constantly on his guard.

After some time a picture of his total situation, his 'world', emerged. He was the only son of elderly parents who had withdrawn into a life of comparative isolation. Apart from his mother's sister, whom they rarely saw, no relatives lived in the same town. He spoke of his parents' silent battles, the roots of which he never understood. They seemed very caring for his well-being and education, and he believed they loved him. He was, so to speak, the common ground on which they met, and he felt some undefined responsibility for their relationship.

Physical affection was rarely shown in this small family, and Tom was concerned with 'keeping himself to himself' in order not to be overwhelmed by unexpressed emotions. He had few friends, partly because he was reluctant to leave his parents alone. An attempt to have a relationship with a girl came to grief because he found any kind of physical contact very difficult. Several times he had been to visit prostitutes.

These are only a few strands in Tom's tightly controlled life, the boundaries of which seemed to be ruled by the double-headed rule 'don't touch – don't be touched'. 'Touched' here is meant both in its literal and its metaphorical sense. This does not mean that there is a causal connection between the nature of Tom's upbringing and the development of his skin condition; many people have similar experiences when they are children without suffering from eczema. But the exploration of Tom's total situation showed a pattern of emotional and physical separation and withdrawal in which the body participated through the skin – the skin being the boundary between a person and his or her surrounding world.

The clarification of his situation helped Tom to relate more understandingly to his skin. His eczema flared up less violently but it did not disappear.

There has been recently a great deal of thought and research into the connection between consciousness and the brain – another area of the mind–body question. The state of present thinking has been most lucidly summarized by John Searle (1995) in the *New York Review of Books*. It seems to be generally believed that brain processes cause consciousness, but not reductively. In other words, consciousness cannot be explained in terms of brain processes, but consciousness is an 'emergent quality' for which these processes are a necessary condition. Searle emphasizes that we do not at present know how this 'causation', this bridging of the gap between neurobiological processes and conscious experience, comes about. It seems to me that it might be helpful to drop the assumption of a causal connection and see consciousness as a total situation in which both physical and non-physical processes are involved.

For the phenomenologist, as we have seen at various places in this book, this gap does not exist, as body and mind are seen as different aspects of the same experience – the experience of the one always implying the experience of the other. This means, however, that all conditions which articulate themselves as psychological disturbances have also physical aspects, even if these remain in the background. Similarly, all physical illness is also emotionally charged – people suffering from flu may be depressed, and people suffering from multiple sclerosis may often strike us as surprisingly optimistic. Again it is important to avoid simple causal explanations, like 'physical suffering is depressing' or 'some medication makes you feel high'. A clarification of the total situation might show us a meaningful connection between the physical phenomenon and its emotional 'attunement', to use Heidegger's expression.

Another consequence of this way of looking at the relation between mind and body is that one cannot rule out the effectiveness of a physical remedy in the case of a psychological disturbance. Psychotherapists tend to be sceptical about the use of physical remedies, or completely reject them. Our experience with the physical treatment of psychological disturbances is not encouraging, and some of it is clearly damaging. But if the disturbance concerns both mind and body we need to remain open to the possibility that both mental and physical approaches may have access to it. Perhaps methods helping towards relaxation and a greater awareness of the physical aspects of our being point to the possibility of a more two-sided approach.

References

Boss, M. (1963) *Psychoanalysis and Daseinsanalysis*. New York: Basic Books.

Cottingham, J. (1993) *A Descartes Dictionary*. Oxford: Blackwell.

Freud, S. (1909) *Notes upon a Case of Obsessional Neurosis*. S.E. I. London: Hogarth Press. (Pelican Freud Library. Vol. 9. Harmondsworth: Penguin Books.)

Freud, S. (1914) *On Narcissism: an Introduction*. S.E. XIV. London: Hogarth Press. (Pelican Freud Library. Vol. 11. Harmondsworth: Penguin Books.)

Freud, S. (1917) *Introductory Lectures on Psycho-Analysis*. S.E. XVI. London: Hogarth Press. (Pelican Freud Library. Vol. 1. Harmondsworth: Penguin Books.)

Freud, S. (1950) *Project for a Scientific Psychology*. S.E. I. London: Hogarth Press.

Merleau-Ponty, M. (1962) *The Phenomenology of Perception*. Tr. C. Smith. London: Routledge & Kegan Paul.

Moore, B.E. and Fine, B.D. (1990) *Psychoanalytic Terms and Concepts*. New Haven, CT: American Psychoanalytic Association.

Searle, J. (1995) 'The history of consciousness', *New York Review of Books* (2 and 16 November).

Smith, D.L. (1992) 'On the eve of a revolution; Freud's concepts of consciousness and unconsciousness in "Studies on hysteria" and the "Project for a scientific psychology"', *British Journal of Psychotherapy*, 9(2): 150–6.

Smith, D.L. (1995) 'Mind and body in Freud', *British Journal of Psychotherapy*, 11(3): 392–7.

Spinoza, B. (1985) *The Collected Works*. Tr. E. Curley. Princeton, NJ: Princeton University Press.

7

Aspects of Anxiety and Guilt

Anxiety

A distinction is generally made between fear and anxiety. Fear is seen as having a definite object; we are afraid of something concrete – the death of a friend, the outcome of a business transaction, the effect of a hurricane. Anxiety, on the other hand, is more free-floating; it is a feeling of apprehension without a specific target, a foreboding that something fearful is going to happen. The distinction is, in fact, not always easy to make. Anxiety is like fear – 'intentional'. As phenomenologists would say, anxiety is always directed towards something. But we may not necessarily know what that something is.

Etymologically, anxiety is an interesting word. It is derived from the Latin *'angere'* which means 'to squeeze, to strangle'. Thus the physical aspect of the emotional state of anxiety is part of the original word meaning. This is also the case in German where *'Angst'* has the stem *'ang'* which means 'narrow, tight'. The same stem is again present in 'anguish'. Etymologically, the body–mind split has not taken place – restriction, tightness and strangulation are the physical aspects of an emotional state. Equally illuminating is the connection between anguish and anger – the same common stem *'ang'* points to the physical and emotional aspects of 'choking' which anger and anguish share. Phenomenologically anxiety and anger are often observed together as ingredients of the same experience.

For the therapist, anxiety in a variety of manifestations is part of what most clients bring into their sessions, and frequently it seems to be their predominant problem. Freud formulated at least two different views about its origin:

1 In the beginning, he described it as 'the universally current coinage for which *any* affective impulse is or can be exchanged

if the ideational content attached to it is subjected to repression' (Freud, 1917: 403–4 [1: 452]). For instance sexual wishes which cannot be owned are repressed, but the feelings about these wishes (shame, resentment, disgust) are experienced as anxiety. Thus, anxiety is the consequence of repression.

2 Later Freud saw anxiety as a kind of 'red light' – a signal of impending danger, a warning. Anything that disturbs the psychic equilibrium creates anxiety: the experience of birth; separation from important figures; instinctual pressures – both sexual and aggressive; the demands of the super-ego.

An existential-phenomenological view sees anxiety not as the result of a psychological mechanism but as an inevitable aspect of existence itself. However, I think it is important to consider both the existential aspect of anxiety and the particular way in which we individually experience it.

The way in which we respond to existential 'givens' depends on the experiential pattern we have developed throughout our life. For instance early and continuing experiences of intense threat and insecurity will give an anxious 'tuning' to our way of experiencing the world. We may focus on catastrophic possibilities and live in constant anxious anticipation. This is not the direct effect of an earlier anxious-making event but an experientially rooted inclination to respond to life anxiously. Such a view will help us to understand individual differences in the experience of anxiety that can sometimes take the form of paralysing panic attacks.

At the same time, anxiety is not the outcome of our individual (ontic) development but an (ontological) aspect of existence itself. The ground for the inevitability of existential anxiety has been discussed by Heidegger (1962) and other existential philosophers at great length and can be summed up as follows:

(a) anxiety is rooted in our 'thrownness' into a world we did not choose;
(b) anxiety is rooted in the necessity to make choices (and even to make no choice is a choice), the outcomes of which are never certain and always imply the rejection of alternatives;
(c) anxiety is rooted in the realization that life is inevitably moving towards death.

Anxiety is in itself neither positive nor negative. It is, in Kierkegaard's words, 'the giddiness of freedom' (1980: 61). In a world where so much is 'facticity' and outside our control, anxiety makes us aware of our possibilities. It is, so to speak, the price we pay for that freedom.

ILLUSTRATION

Joan's life was haunted by anxieties. Whenever anyone – her husband, her teenage son, a friend – did not arrive at the time she expected them, she thought they must have had an accident. She would not touch food unless it was absolutely fresh. Any mark on her skin, any physical symptom – even a cough – spelt severe illness. She was well aware of the irrationality of her fears and was constantly engaged in a fight against her forebodings. Sometimes she won the fight and there was peace for a while. At other times anxiety paralysed her, and she was unable to do anything as long as she lacked concrete proof that her fear was unjustified. This shows the difficulty of distinguishing clearly between anxiety and fear: Joan was aware of the dubious nature of her fears – but were the objects of her concern less 'concrete' for being imaginary?

In our talks it became clear that it was Joan's mother who, early on, had introduced Joan into her own anxious world. The little girl had to present herself every morning before going to school so that mother could feel her forehead to find out whether she had a fever. She was not allowed to go on school outings or participate in games. The message of mother's world was: life is dangerous, do not expose yourself, protect yourself, always expect the worst!

Mother's anxiety cannot be called the cause of Joan's continual apprehension. Joan had been gradually educated into an anxious self-protective way of relating to the world, and she had been clearly willing to learn this lesson. (I have worked with other clients who in answer to similar influences became adventurous and even reckless!) Other factors, like her father's frequent absence, contributed. The grip of her anxiety pattern only loosened when she came to see that, paradoxically, her refusal to accept life's potential riskiness made her perceive risks everywhere.

Guilt

Unlike anxiety, the word 'guilt' has little to offer etymologically. It is an Old English word of unknown origin and seems to have originally meant 'crime, offence', and only later came to describe the feelings engendered by offending actions. The word is related to the German word for money – *'Geld'*. But more importantly the German word for guilt, which is *'Schuld'*, means both guilt and debt – and this wider sense of 'indebtedness' comes closest to the existential sense of guilt, as we shall see.

Freud saw guilt as a reaction to the often-punishing judgement of the 'super-ego', an internalization of parental but also socio-cultural convention and authority. Being dominated by super-ego forces is not unlike 'falling' into the clutches of Heidegger's *'das Man'* (usually translated as 'the they'). Our 'fallenness' tells us what to do and overlays the 'voice of conscience', which Heidegger calls a 'primordial phenomenon' (1962). The 'voice of conscience' calls us back from the denial and avoidance of the 'givens' of Being.

Freud does not seem to distinguish between super-ego and conscience. Thus psychoanalysis does not concern itself with feelings of *real* guilt, which we experience when we have in fact done wrong. Buber gives us the example 'of a man's betrayal of his friend or a cause' (Buber, 1965: 117). Psychoanalysis instead focuses on guilt *feelings*, our unjustified reactions to the dictates of internalized voices of authority. These 'guilt feelings' need to be distinguished from feelings of *real* guilt – 'existential guilt' as Buber calls it. But there is a more concise meaning to this term. This is clearly expressed by Boss: 'Man's existential guilt consists in his failing to carry out the mandate to fulfil all his possibilities' (1963: 270). 'Thrown' into a world which is already there and unchosen, human being *(Dasein)* has the freedom to project itself into the future by realizing its possibilities – or failing to do so. *Dasein* will, of course, never be able to do this completely and will, therefore, always lag behind its possibilities. Existential guilt is thus an inevitable aspect of existence.

In talking about guilt, an aspect of psychological disturbance never absent though sometimes concealed, we need to distinguish between:

(a)   unfounded ('neurotic') guilt feelings,
(b)   real guilt which needs to be faced; and
(c)   existential guilt which has to be seen as an intrinsic aspect of existence itself.

In therapeutic situations it is not always easy to make these distinctions.

ILLUSTRATION

Sheila thinks of herself as fundamentally 'bad'. Her mother was very strict – 'she had to be, I was quite out of control'. Sheila is a middle-aged woman and works as a secretary. She is efficient and earns a good salary. She lives on her own, a few attempts at making relationships having failed. Her conviction that she is 'bad' and her loneliness is a punishment which she deserves remains insufficiently explained.

There is one childhood memory, however, that seems central to the way she sees herself. When she was seven years old she coveted a little doll in the window of a toyshop near where she lived. Mother refused to buy it for her. So she took some money from her mother's purse, which was kept on the shelf in the kitchen. However, the owner of the shop became suspicious and asked mother whether it was alright for Sheila to buy the doll. At this juncture Sheila's story becomes confused – but there seems to have been a terrific showdown with her mother calling her a thief who would never amount to anything and would end in prison. The important point is that Sheila entirely sided with her mother, and, even more importantly, she still feels that this event proves her wickedness and that what she remembers as her punishment – not being allowed to leave her room for a whole week – was completely just.

This story shows how difficult it is to separate out the various aspects of guilt. On the face of it, mother's strict moral code has become part of herself – in Freudian terms it has become an aspect of her super-ego. In existential-phenomenological terms it would also be possible to see her as the victim of Heidegger's das Man, the sociocultural norm which considers taking money from somebody's purse a theft, whatever the circumstances. And does not a girl of seven know that taking money is wrong, and has not her feeling of guilt, exaggerated and distorted though it may be, an element of reality?

Such considerations were of little help to her. We had to explore the total situation of a little girl who found herself imprisoned in a moralistic, unloving world and made some desperate attempt to break out of it. The story of the stolen money can be understood in this way – the failure of her attempt to break free leading to an even more passionate identification with the prison to which she had to return. It was only when she could understand her 'trespasses' as attempts to 'break through' that her oppressive guilt feelings began to weaken. This took a long time.

There is clearly a connection between the existential aspects of guilt and anxiety. Confronted with the freedom of choice we may feel 'giddiness', to use Kierkegaard's term, and try to avoid choosing altogether. Not to make a choice is, as we have already said, also a choice; but it will leave us with the feeling of 'indebtedness', with existential guilt.

References

Boss, M. (1963) *Psychoanalysis and Daseinsanalysis*. New York: Basic Books.

Buber, M. (1965) 'Guilt and guilt feelings', in M. Friedman (ed.), *The Knowledge of Man*. New York: Humanities Press International Inc.

Freud, S. (1917) *Introductory Lectures on Psycho-Analysis*. S.E. XVI. London: Hogarth Press. (Pelican Freud Library. Vol. 1. Harmondsworth: Penguin Books.)

Heidegger, M. (1962) *Being and Time*. Tr. J. Macquarrie and E. Robinson. Oxford: Blackwell.

Kierkegaard, S. (1980) *The Concept of Anxiety*. Tr. R. Thomte. Princeton, NJ: Princeton University Press.

8

The Question of the Unconscious

In *A Note on the Unconscious in Psycho-Analysis*, Freud writes:

> Unconsciousness seemed to us at first only an enigmatical characteristic of a definite psychical act. Now it means more for us. It is a sign that this act partakes of the nature of a certain psychical category known to us by other and more important characters and that it belongs to a system of psychical activity which is deserving of our fullest attention. . . . The system revealed by the sign that the single acts forming part of it are unconscious we designate by the name 'The Unconscious', for want of a better and less ambiguous term. (Freud, 1912: 266 [11: 57])

The last sentence of this passage contains a *non sequitur*: the move from the adjective 'unconscious' to the noun 'The Unconscious' which is called a 'system'. It is this move from 'unconscious' to 'The Unconscious' which gives rise to a phenomenological critique. That we are not aware of something now which we have been aware of before and may be aware of again is an undeniable phenomenon. But that 'the forgotten' has meanwhile been put away into a part of the mind which is called 'The Unconscious' is an explanation that does not necessarily follow.

Freud had a number of reasons which led him to propose this theory. He was concerned with presenting psychoanalysis as scientific, and at the time science was still dominated by the Cartesian assumption that the world could be explained by the laws of Newtonian physics. But more specifically, Freud was influenced by the ideas of the physicist and philosopher G.T. Fechner. Fechner believed all psychic phenomena are measurable and it was he who introduced the concept of 'psychic locality'.

'The Unconscious' is such a 'psychic locality'. Freud, it must be said, was by no means always at ease with this spatial mode of presentation. In his lecture, 'Resistance and Repression' in the *Introductory Lectures on Psycho-Analysis*, Freud describes 'the system of the unconscious' in the following way:

> Let us . . . compare the system of the unconscious to a large entrance hall, in which the mental impulses jostle one another like separate individuals. Adjoining this entrance hall there is a second, narrower room – a kind of drawing-room – in which consciousness, too, resides. But on the threshold between these two rooms a watchman performs his function: he examines the different mental impulses, acts as a censor, and will not admit them into the drawing-room if they displease him.

Freud adds to this description:

> Now I know you will say that these ideas are both crude and fantastic and quite impermissible in a scientific account. I know that they are crude: and more than that, I know that they are incorrect, and, if I am not very much mistaken, I already have something better to take their place. (1917: 295–6 [1: 336–7]

Whatever Freud had in mind has not emerged, but it is important to realize that at one time he called his mechanistic description of 'repression', which is so much part of any psychodynamic approach, 'crude' and 'incorrect'.

If Freud's description is 'impermissible' as 'a scientific account', it is equally questionable phenomenologically. For 'The Unconscious' is not a phenomenon, it cannot be experienced as such, but its existence can only be inferred, and inferences may be accurate but can also be false.

Why has this concept been so readily accepted? It is, I think, an answer to our fear of gaps, our need for unbroken causal chains holding our world together: whatever is here now, then no longer, and then perhaps here again, must have gone somewhere, must have hidden somewhere while it was not present. The notion of 'The Unconscious' is indeed 'fantastic', as Freud calls it – a phantasy about a hidden link that keeps our fear of experiential gaps at bay.

Prereflective and reflective consciousness

Rejecting the concept of an unconscious psychic locality, phenomenologists still need to account for states of awareness and unawareness, and they see them as aspects of consciousness itself. Sartre distinguishes between prereflective and reflective consciousness. But Sartre's view of consciousness – which was to him a central characteristic of the human subject – is different to that of Freud. Betty Cannon puts this very clearly: 'Unlike Freud, Sartre views consciousness as all of a piece, without compartments or spheres. Reflective consciousness is simply prereflective consciousness turning and making an object of its own (past) actions, feelings, and gestures'. She continues: 'Consciousness for Sartre is not a thing with substance and structure, as the psyche is for Freud . . . It is an openness towards Being, a *desire* or *lack* of a future fullness rather than a self-contained, intrapsychic system' (Cannon, 1991: 38). We are reminded of Heidegger's view of existence as *Dasein*, as 'a sphere of the potentiality of perception and awareness' (Heidegger, 1987: 4).

Cannon provides a lucid illustration of the relation between reflective and prereflective consciousness:

> Take, for example, the alcoholic who says that he or she wishes to stop drinking but simply cannot do so. On a reflective level, this person believes that alcohol is ruining his or her life. On a prereflective level, the glass of whisky beckons in the form of a future state of intoxication which one desires. . . . Thus we come to understand that for this client to cease to reach for the glass of whisky (or the addictive relationship or the work project) will mean a willingness to face an intolerable longing. (1991: 48)

We can say that in a therapy based on these ideas, reflecting on the unreflected takes the place of making the unconscious conscious.

The process of dissociation

Echoing Sartre's distinction between a prereflective and a reflective consciousness, Ernesto Spinelli (1994: 154 ff.) proposes a theory of 'dissociation' to account for the phenomena which the psychoanalytic concept of the unconscious tries to explain. Spinelli bases his ideas on Braude's (1991) philosophical explorations of multiple personality and Hilgard's (1986) comparison between notions of dissociation and repression.

Human beings, in this view, have the capacity to dissociate their awareness from experiences, not only when they cannot accept them but also when they become irrelevant to the present focus of their attention. It is not difficult to see that without this capacity we would be swamped by impressions, sensations and experiences. Unlike repression, dissociation can by no means be seen as pathogenic as such.

Psychotherapists will be more concerned with the form of dissociation which, as 'denial', turns away from sensations, desires or experiences which are unacceptable or intolerable. 'Denial' is, of course, a psychoanalytic term used by Freud and described as a 'defence mechanism'. But unlike 'repression' it does not immediately conjure up the image of an unconscious locality. In fact for Freud, denial (or 'negation' as Strachey has translated 'Verneinung') 'is the intellectual substitute for repression', and is as such a conscious process. It 'is a way of taking cognizance of what is repressed; indeed it is already a lifting of repression, though not, of course, an acceptance of what is repressed' (Freud, 1925: 235–6 [11: 438]). For Freud what is denied is always the reappearance of what is repressed. For the existential therapist the whole process – dissociation and the rejection or integration of what has been dissociated – takes place within consciousness.

From this existential perspective, the conflict our clients bring into therapy is not considered to be between the conscious mind and the disturbing force of unaccepted and unacceptable desires pressing upwards from an unconscious into which they have been repressed. It is between the way we have defined ourselves, our 'self-construct' as Spinelli calls it, and the way we experience ourselves when it does not 'match' our definition. This definition is the outcome of past experience as well as sociocultural circumstances. It can become fixed so that new experiences have to be disowned – 'this is not really me' – and the clash between what I believe myself to be and what I experience myself being manifests itself as psychological disturbance (Spinelli, 1994: 345 ff.).

ILLUSTRATION

John is a young man managing a department in a reputable bookshop. He had a conventional upbringing and hopes to marry soon and have a family. He has a steady girlfriend who works as a secretary at a publisher's. About a year ago he met a girl at an office party, an art student who works temporarily in the art department. He describes how she invited him home after the party – 'it is the kind of thing I never do' – and 'seduced' him. Since then they have been having an affair. Recently he has developed sensations of anxiety – his heart beats fast, there are outbreaks of sweating. 'Sleeping with two girls is just not me', he says. He has come into therapy because he 'needs help with making a choice'.

After a comparatively short time it becomes clear that he has, in fact, made a choice – the choice of having two relationships, each of which offers something different. His sexual relationship with his girlfriend is sporadic and unsatisfactory but they have similar interests, go to the theatre together, read the same books. With the other girl he has 'a lot of fun', 'sex is very good', they 'laugh a lot'. There is thus a conflict between his 'self-construct' – 'I am a serious responsible man who will be faithful to his girlfriend, marry her and have children with her' – and the new experience of enjoying an uncommitted sexual relationship. He has tried to deal with it by considering it as 'alien' to himself, 'dissociating' the experience. He needs to broaden the definition of himself by including his sexual desire and need for fun – only then will he be able to make a choice for one or the other relationship, if such a choice seems then necessary to him.

In Sartrean terms we might say that John's sexual needs and love of fun remains unreflected – though not unconscious – and thus he can deceive himself into believing that he is the kind of person who cannot be unfaithful to the woman he intends to marry. The task of the therapist is then to help the client to reflect the unreflected.

Being-in-the-world

In the existential-phenomenological approach to questions arising from the concept of 'the unconscious', the emphasis can be on the phenomenological *or* the existential elements which – as we have seen – are not the same. At the risk of over-simplification we could say that phenomenology – as created by Husserl – is concerned with consciousness, the conscious act which is intentional and has a phenomenon as its object. As Solomon puts it: 'the phenomenon is inseparably connected to experience, for it is a phenomenon because it is an object experienced' (Solomon, 1987: 171).

Existentialism does not, in the same way, focus on consciousness as such – it is concerned with man's being as 'Being-in-the-world'. For this reason existential philosophers cannot accept Husserl's 'reduction': 'One cannot "bracket existence" as the *epoche* requires; our existence and the existence of the world around us are given together as the starting point of all phenomenological description' (Solomon, 1987: 179). We can say that Sartre's and Spinelli's critiques of the unconscious are essentially phenomenological, replacing the 'psychic locality' underlying consciousness by a differentiation of consciousness itself. Medard Boss's approach is more clearly indebted to Heidegger's concept of 'Being-in-the-world'. In common with Sartre and Spinelli, Boss rejects 'the usual objectifying capsule-like representations of a psyche', to use Heidegger's words (1987: 3), in which the unconscious is part of a structure underlying conscious experience. Being-in-the-world is a relational state and human beings are always part of a context which includes the world and others. All experience is experience of this context, and any disturbance is a distortion or crippling of such an experience.

As we have seen, human existence responds to specific characteristics of Being like relatedness, spatiality and embodiment, and this response is inevitably informed by circumstances and past experience. Thus, for example, agoraphobia and claustrophobia are 'an obstructive impairment in the spatiality of people' (Boss, 1979: 216) who are threatened by too much or too little space. Such impaired 'being-in-the-world' is not rooted in an intrapsychic conflict but 'out there' in the interaction between us and our world.

There is literally no 'space' for the concept of an 'unconscious' within a perspective which sees existence as the relatedness between persons and their world. As Boss puts it: 'analysis of *Dasein* enables us to become aware that the things and fellow men which an individual encounters appear to him within the meaning-disclosing light of his *Dasein* immediately . . . as what they are, according to the world-openness of his existence' (Boss, 1963: 93/4). At a later point he adds: 'if we do not depart from the immediate experience of what is commonly called an idea or psychic representation of something, we need no construct of an unconscious in the sense of an inner psychic locality' (Boss, 1963: 96). We call this approach 'daseinsanalytic' – 'Dasein' (being there) being Heidegger's understanding of human existence as an opening 'to all that encounters and addresses it' (Heidegger, 1987: 3). This approach was elaborated by Medard Boss and underlies the concerns and activities of the Daseinsanalytische Institute in Zürich. It could perhaps be summarized in the following way:

1   Awareness is not awareness of something within a 'psyche' situated inside ourselves, but awareness of things and persons that are with us in the world. Even when I am thinking of someone who is not physically present, I am with him and not with some 'inner representation' of him. Physical being-with is only one aspect of being-in-the-world.

2   It is the quality of our engagement with what appears to us in the world that determines the degree of our awareness. If we are no longer aware of what appears to us, it has not gone away to some intra-psychic place from where it might return. *Our* awareness has moved away from it, *we* have disengaged ourselves.

3   We frequently refuse to engage ourselves with what appears to us. Previous experiences may have narrowed our mode of experiencing so that we are not open to what we meet. Anxiety in the face of the unfamiliar, clinging to protective dependencies and the fear of disintegration and annihilation may lead to a denial of what shows itself.

ILLUSTRATION

Charles feels compelled to wash his hands a great many times a day. If he is prevented from doing so, he becomes extremely anxious. In therapy he reveals an overwhelming fear of germs which he admits to finding irrational but cannot master. In a number of talks, he speaks about his difficulty in making decisions as he can never be certain what the right decision is. Not to make a decision at all seems safest, particularly when an important issue has to be decided.

Charles's whole life is haunted by the fear of taking a wrong step or committing himself firmly to a course of action. Life is full of threats that need to be avoided, germs are part of these. Eventually he comes to see that he has embarked on an impossible quest – the quest for absolute security.

Psychoanalytic explanations of compulsive symptoms are complex and may involve the client's hatred of his father which turns into the phantasy of the father's hatred of the client, and eventually into a feeling of universal threat. An existential approach would see these symptoms as a flight from the unavoidable insecurity which is a 'given' of human existence.

References

Boss, M. (1963) *Psychoanalysis and Daseinsanalysis*. New York: Basic Books.

Boss, M. (1979) *Existential Foundations of Medicine and Psychology*. Tr. S. Conway and A. Cleaves. Northvale, NJ: Jason Aronson.

Cannon, B. (1991) *Sartre and Psychoanalysis. An Existentialist Challenge to Clinical Metatheory*. Kansas: University Press of Kansas.

Freud, S. (1912) *A Note on the Unconscious in Psycho-Analysis*. S.E. XII. London: Hogarth Press. (Pelican Freud Library. Vol. 11. Harmondsworth: Penguin Books.)

Freud, S. (1917) *Introductory Lectures on Psycho-Analysis*. S.E. XVI. London: Hogarth Press. (Pelican Freud Library. Vol. 1. Harmondsworth: Penguin Books.)

Freud, S. (1925) *Negation*. S.E. XIX. London: Hogarth Press. (Pelican Freud Library. Vol. 11. Harmondsworth: Penguin Books.)

Heidegger, M. (1987) *Zollikoner Seminare, Protokolle – Gespräche – Briefe*. Ed. M. Boss. Frankfurt a.M.: Klostermann.

Solomon, R.S. (1987) *From Hegel to Existentialism*. Oxford: Oxford University Press.

Spinelli, E. (1994) *Demystifying Therapy*. London: Constable.

9

Dreams and Symptoms

It may seem strange that I have decided to address dreams and symptoms in the same chapter. However, we have already seen that Freud viewed them as the result of similar processes: rejected and unfulfilled wishes which had been repressed into the unconscious returning into consciousness in disguise – either in our sleep as dreams or 'neurotically' as symptoms. (A third mode of masked return is inappropriate behaviour – *'Fehlleistungen'* which has been absurdly translated as 'parapraxis' – like lapses of memory or saying the opposite of what one wanted to say.)

Dreams and symptoms are both phenomena, contents of our experience. Freud felt that phenomena should 'yield in importance' to those forces behind them that brought them about. Thus dreams and symptoms need to be interpreted in order to reveal their meaning. Interpretation implies for Freud an exploration of the origin of the phenomena and their replacement by what they represent. Thus a handbag in your dream, or an obsessional thought in your mind, do not mean what they are but represent something else that analysis needs to discover. We have seen that for the existential-phenomenological therapist, phenomena 'yield in importance' to nothing and mean what they are, though they may mean more than is immediately apparent.

The interpretation of dreams and symptoms means phenomenologically viewing them in their widest possible context which includes the story and experiential framework of the dreaming or suffering person.

Dreams

'According to Freud, the function of dreams is to preserve sleep by representing wishes as fulfilled which could otherwise waken the dreamer' (Rycroft, 1995: 41). The important aspect of this explanation – which psychoanalysis did not, of course, maintain in this simplistic form – is its view of dreams as essentially protective, aiding the denial and disguise of disturbing impulses. Thus each dream has a twofold nature: the 'manifest' (that is phenomenal) dream is the disguise which hides the 'latent' (that is 'real') dream content. Dreams, therefore, cannot be taken at face value as their 'real' meaning is not apparent.

Not all psychoanalytically orientated therapists follow this conceptualization. Charles Rycroft for instance, in his significantly titled book *The Innocence of Dreams*, opposed Freud's characterization of dreams as 'abnormal psychical phenomena' and proposes that 'imagination is a natural, normal activity of an agent or self, and that dreaming is its sleeping form'. He, like others, does not wish to see dreams reduced to concealing disguises of psychological disturbances but stresses their creative potentiality: 'If dreams have meaning and can be interpreted, they must be creations of a person or agent who endows them with meaning' (Rycroft, 1979: 4–5).

The phemonenologist instead of distinguishing between surface and depth, tries to establish ever-widening contexts. Thus there cannot be a distinction between 'manifest' and 'latent' dream contents. But Boss rightly stresses that existential psychotherapy 'agrees with psychoanalytic experience that those realms of the human world which find admittance into the light of the dreaming *Dasein* are those a human being has not become aware of in his waking state' (Boss, 1963: 262). However, as Boss also emphasizes, dreams are not something we 'have', they are an aspect of our being – 'we are our dreaming state' (1963: 261). They are not puzzles to be solved but openings to be attended to. Dreams are 'an uncovering, an unveiling, and never a covering up or a veiling of a psychic content' (1963: 262). We come close here to Heidegger's definition of truth as 'the unconcealed', which is the meaning of the Greek word '*aletheia*'.

ILLUSTRATION 1

Ted has dreamt that he was walking along the road with an opened umbrella though it was not raining.

Psychoanalytically the umbrella might be seen as an erect penis displayed at an inappropriate time. Does Ted fear for his sexual potency so that he has to demonstrate it even when it is not necessary – or is it the one thing he is certain of so that he has to convince himself at all times that it works? In such an interpretation, the umbrella as such only represents the penis and does not itself play a part in the final understanding of the dream.

Existential-phenomenologically, the umbrella remains what it is – a protective instrument. The dream would raise the question whether Ted feels the need to protect himself even when such a protection does not seem called for. He is unready to face the existential given that complete security is existentially unachievable.

ILLUSTRATION 2

Jim dreamt repeatedly that on a train journey in the company of friends he leaves the train for various reasons, for instance to buy a newspaper or something to eat, and then does not find the train again. Has it left? Is he on the wrong platform? Now he is quite alone and does not know what to do to rejoin his friends.

Jim is a young man who complains that things never go right for him, he constantly 'misses the bus' – so to speak. He loses his girlfriends, does not get the job he applies for. But he never asks himself what his own contributions are to these misfortunes. Looking at these dreams, he discovers with some surprise that his isolation – being separated from his friends – is not something that just 'happened' to him but is a consequence of a move of his own – leaving the train – no matter how innocent that move may have seemed.

In the course of further work, these dreams played an important part in exploring his need always to see himself as the victim of circumstances. He had to answer a challenge coming not from his therapist but from his own dreams.

ILLUSTRATION 3

Rose remembers that when she was about twelve years old she had a night-marish dream which she has never forgotten. She dreamed that her mother woke her up in the middle of the night to show her something. She took her into the garden where she saw with horror that the whole sky was covered by a web of toy aeroplanes. She woke up screaming.

Rose loved aeroplanes as a child and thought they gave human beings the freedom of birds. Her mother was a rigid rule-bound woman, and her father had died when she was very young. One could say that the dream reflected the mother's controlling ways by turning the aeroplanes from being symbols of freedom into the image of a suffocating trap. This would be its ontic meaning, a confrontation with her own specific way of being in the world. But there is perhaps also an ontological reference to the uncontrollable and limiting aspects of Being.

Symptoms

Freud saw the formation of symptoms as a compromise between a repressed impulse and the repressing force that opposes its return into consciousness. The compromise formation – like the manifest dream – disguises and neutralizes the disturbing impulse. Once again the person is protected from the potentially unacceptable consequences of his or her unaccepted wishes. A non-organic paralysis of an arm might be seen as the wish to hit out, which is stopped by a forbidding force.

An existential approach does not reduce a symptom to a conflict of which it is the compromise solution. It tries to understand it in its own right – what it reveals immediately and what it means in the context of the client's life.

ILLUSTRATION 1

Anne's anorexia was understood by her psychodynamically orientated psychotherapist as an attempt to remain a child, by not becoming a sexual being in the eyes of a father on whom she strongly depended as she did not get on very well with her mother.

When she came to see me she was alternating between fasting and over-eating, and was no longer living at home. An apparently directionless series of sessions was given a new impulse by her saying: 'Not eating was the only thing over which I had control at home'. Further exploration showed a conflict between her need to be in control of her life without ever feeling she was, and her fear that her constant self-monitoring killed all spontaneity. Her fasting could be seen as part of her need to be in sole charge, while her overeating could be understood as the equally obsessional need to let go, to be irresponsible. The aim of our common work was an exploration of the possibilities as well as the limits of what human beings can control. The grip of her eating compulsions loosened slowly.

ILLUSTRATION 2

Paul found himself caught in a pattern of unsatisfactory relationships with women. He was a lawyer and involved himself with a number of women colleagues who were somewhat older than himself, successful in their work, and in the end not ready to give up their career while he wished to settle down and have a family. Though he was aware of the pattern, whenever he began a relationship he managed to deceive himself into believing that this time he had found a partner who was ready to commit herself to his own plans for the future.

It did not take us long to find that his own mother played a part in this pattern. She was a successful doctor, and his father a well-known surgeon. Psychodynamically we might see his choice of partners as an unconscious attempt to repeat an Oedipal involvement. Existential therapists, however, do not work on such one-directional assumptions. The concept of existential temporality conceives the past as part of the present – we are what we have become. The past inevitably informs present experience.

Exploring Paul's 'world' we found that he rarely met any woman who did not aim at a professional career – first he met friends of his mother, and later when he was studying to be a lawyer, he met his fellow students. But, more importantly, he was expected to marry such a woman and he never questioned that this was the right thing to do. Whether or not he had had an Oedipal involvement with his mother – he spoke of her rather coolly and seemed not to like her very much – this had to be seen as part of a wider sociocultural context.

This way of looking at Paul's problems offered a possibility of change. Psychological difficulties which seem to be rooted in unresolved developmental hold-ups have a deterministic feel about them. Paul's realization that he did not have to marry a particular kind of woman opened up a choice: he could either continue to seek a partner among women involved in building up a career for themselves and knowing that he might fail, or turn in a different direction altogether. This is often the only thing a therapy can do: open the client's eyes to the possibility of a different choice.

References

Boss, M. (1963) *Psychoanalysis and Daseinsanalysis*. New York: Basic Books.

Rycroft, C. (1979) *The Innocence of Dreams*. Northvale, NJ: Jason Aronson.

Rycroft, C. (1995) *A Critical Dictionary of Psycho-analysis*. 2nd edn. Harmondsworth: Penguin Books.

10
Being-in-the-World Sexually

Sexuality has been strangely neglected by writers on existential psychotherapy. The theme has also remained unfocused in existential thinking. Heidegger does not seem concerned with it. Sartre, in *Being and Nothingness*, states that sexuality is not determined by biological instincts but by one's 'upsurge . . . into a world where "there are" others' (Sartre, 1958: 407) and he characterizes the sexual relationship as 'a double reciprocal incarnation' (1958: 391). This is an evocative phrase but we also know that in Sartre's description relationships tend to slide into a sadomasochistic mode where the battle for superiority and the invalidation of the other is paramount.

It is, not surprisingly, Merleau-Ponty who devotes a chapter in his *Phenomenology of Perception* to our sexual existence, saying that 'in his sexuality is projected [man's] manner of being towards the world, that is, towards time and other men' (Merleau-Ponty, 1962: 158). Madison, in his book on Merleau-Ponty, comments: 'sexuality never functions as an autonomous physiological mechanism. It is already penetrated and transformed through and through by personal attitudes, and conversely personal existence always has a sexual meaning or coloring' (Madison, 1981: 47–8).

Merleau-Ponty sees sexuality as an intrinsic aspect of existence in a way other writers fail to do. But just as 'Being-in-the-world' means implicitly 'Being-with-others', 'Being-towards-death', 'Being-in-the-body', it also means 'Being sexually'. We are all sexual beings and our sexuality, like all existence, has 'given' aspects. It is our responses to these 'given' aspects which vary. An existential-phenomenological approach needs to explore what these 'givens' are and the ways in which we respond. Such an exploration may not be easy but we need to attempt it if we wish to understand the spectrum of sexual difficulties which our clients present to us.

It is interesting to reflect that psychoanalytic therapy had its origin in Freud's speculations on the nature and transformations of the sexual drive, and for some time critics of his theories focused on what they called his 'pan-sexualism'. If writers on existential psychotherapy seem to neglect the sexual aspects of human difficulties – with the exception of Medard Boss who, as we shall see, in dealing with sexuality abandons his phenomenological stance – there may be in this an element of opposition to the psychoanalytic emphasis on the sexual drive.

Sexual difference

Anatomically and physiologically, men and women find themselves in the realm of the 'given'. But anatomical and physiological differences have given rise to sociocultural assumptions which do not necessarily follow. These assumptions may present themselves as 'givens' when, in fact, they are not. The danger that biology is seen as 'destiny' is always with us, in spite of feminism's untiring opposition. In Western culture, for instance, men are considered to be more active, more aggressive, more reasonable than women; being a woman implies being more passive, less aggressive, more emotional. Such a view proposes unilinear causal connections between our anatomy and physiology and our way of being which entirely ignores context and history. It is, therefore, unphenomenological.

It is interesting to consider Freud's views on this matter. Freud has often been accused, and rightly, of being ambivalent and confused in his approach to sexual difference, but he could also be astonishingly open-minded. In his *Three Essays on the Theory of Sexuality* (published in 1905) he proposed that the sexual drive is always masculine, in both boys and girls. But in a footnote, written ten years later, he explains that it is difficult to distinguish what the terms 'masculine' and 'feminine' actually mean. Pure masculinity and femininity cannot be found, there is always a 'mixture' (Freud, 1905: 219–20 [7: 141–2]). In *Civilization and its Discontents*, Freud asserts that man has an 'unmistakably bisexual disposition'. Anatomically, maleness and femaleness can be clearly characterized, but not psychologically (Freud, 1930: 105–6 [12: 295–6]). Freud, in his papers on sexuality, frequently returns to the notion of constitutional bisexuality, which stands like a question mark on the margins of those aspects of his theories which tend to polarize femininity and masculinity.

Such a polarization of masculinity and femininity arises from the concept of the Oedipus complex where anatomy seems indeed to become destiny. This complex, briefly summed up, implies that the boy's desire of mother and envy of father leads to a fear of castration which can only be held at bay by renunciation of mother and identification with father. Here the fear of the loss of the penis, the agent and symbol of masculinity, is central to the progress of male development. This identification with father becomes the basis of the formation of the super-ego. Initially Freud thought that the process he called the Oedipus complex applied to women as well. When it came to a closer understanding of the psychological processes involved, Freud felt at a loss and said so quite openly. Ernest Jones reports him saying once to the psychoanalyst Marie Bonaparte: 'The great question that has never been answered and which I have not yet been able to answer, despite my thirty years of research into the feminine soul, is "what do women want?"' (Jones, 1961: 474). As late as 1926, in *The Question of Lay Analysis*, Freud wrote: 'We know less about the sexual life of little girls than of boys. But we need not feel ashamed of this distinction; after all, the sexual life of adult women is a "dark continent" for psychology' (1926: 212).

Eventually Freud admitted that the same theory that applied to men could not be applied to women. There could not be a threat of castration when castration has already taken place, so to speak. So what is the little girl's reason for renouncing father? And why did she turn away from mother and towards father in the first place? Freud proposes the following sequence of events: the little girl discovers that she has no penis; she holds mother responsible for this lack which she resents and turns to father. 'She gives up her wish for a penis and puts in place of it a wish for a child: and *with that purpose in view* she takes her father as a love-object' (Freud, 1925: 256 [7: 340]). But the girl is disappointed once more: 'One has an impression that the Oedipus complex is then gradually given up because this wish is never fulfilled' (Freud, 1924: 179 [7: 321]). Freud does not clearly state what happens in the end: 'It must be admitted that in general our insight into these developmental processes in girls is unsatisfactory, incomplete and vague' (1924: 179 [7: 321]).

What happens to the formation of the super-ego in these circumstances? Freud knows that he is treading on thin ice when he says: 'I cannot evade the notion (though I hesitate to give it expression) that for women the level of what is ethically normal is different from what it is in men. Their super-ego is never so inexorable, so impersonal, so independent of its emotional origins as we require it to be in men' (Freud, 1925: 257 [7: 342]).

These theoretical constructions seem, to some extent, far-fetched despite their undoubted ingenuity. But constructions are not phenomena – they remain inexperienced, do not 'meet the eye'. Why do I devote space to them? The fact that Freud experienced such difficulties in imposing his rather inflexible schema on the ever-changing spectrum of what we call masculinity and femininity illustrates very strikingly the difference between intellectual explanation and experiential perception. (One has to read Freud's various attempts to 'explain' gender differences offered in the papers he produced throughout his life to appreciate his difficulties!)

But for psychotherapists, an examination of the Oedipal schema is particularly important if they wish to assess the psychoanalytic contribution to the question of homosexuality.

Homosexuality

Freud's attitude towards homosexuality was ambivalent throughout. Though he clearly denied that it was the 'disorder' it is still considered to be by a number of psychoanalytically orientated therapists, his theories nevertheless contributed greatly to the common assumption that it is a developmental arrest. This is, in fact, what Freud called it himself in the famous letter he wrote answering the enquiries of the mother of a homosexual man. This letter is entirely sympathetic, speaks of the 'great injustice to persecute homosexuality' and mentions Plato, Michaelangelo and Leonardo da Vinci as great men who had been homosexuals. But it also calls homosexuality 'a variation of the sexual function produced by a certain arrest of sexual development' (Jones, 1961: 624).

Clearly this statement has its roots in the concept of the 'negative Oedipus complex', which finds its solution in the identification of the boy with his mother and the girl with her father. In other words, there is a 'normal' development – the identification with the parent of the same sex – which makes its alternative 'abnormal'. Another assumption of this theory is that identification with the parent of the other sex implies the search for a partner of the same sex, which does not follow. As therapists we frequently see clients who are over-involved with the parent of the other sex and are nevertheless heterosexual. (Psychoanalysts would perhaps say that they are homosexual but do not know it.)

On the other hand, in *The Ego and the Super-Ego*, Freud – returning to his proposition that all human beings are basically bisexual – stresses constitutional elements: 'In both sexes the relative strength of the masculine and feminine sexual dispositions is what determines whether the outcome of the Oedipus situation shall be an identification with the father or with the mother' (Freud, 1923: 33 [11: 372]). But how can a development be called arrested when it depends on constitutional disposition? In the same passage, Freud wonders whether we should not assume the existence of a:

> more complete Oedipus complex, which is twofold, positive and negative, and is due to the bisexuality originally present in children: that is to say, a boy has not merely an ambivalent attitude towards his father and an affectionate object-choice towards his mother, but at the same time he also behaves like a girl and displays an affectionate feminine attitude to his father and a corresponding jealousy and hostility towards his mother. (1923: 33)

In other words, a clear developmental distinction between heterosexuality and homosexuality cannot, in fact, be made. In writing this, Freud is much nearer to a phenomenological view of sexual difference than in his psychoanalytic speculations.

It would, of course, be absurd to say that psychoanalytic theory is responsible for the widespread hostility which homosexuality arouses in our culture. It is more likely that the theory mirrors the culture. The reasons make up a web of many strands and to follow their ramifications would take us beyond the scope of this book. But at the centre of this web is a concept of 'nature' which is a

system of arbitrarily fixed sociocultural rules. A primitive biological view – which to some extent is also reflected by some
religious beliefs – sees the exclusive aim of sexuality as procreation. Homosexuality cannot be 'natural' because it cannot lead
to childbirth. Thus sexual feelings and acts that are not directed
towards procreation are necessarily 'unnatural'. Such a view, of
course, restricts severely the occasions on which heterosexuality
can be called natural. An existential-phenomenological perspective cannot accept the imposition of such an inflexible sociocultural
grid – without any regard for interaction, history or context – on
existence.

Early on, in his *Three Essays on the Theory of Sexuality*, Freud
contradicted this biological view of homosexuality by denying its
innateness. 'Under a great number of conditions and in surprisingly numerous individuals, the nature and importance of the
sexual object recedes into the background' (Freud, 1905: 149 [7:
61]). In a footnote, added in 1910, Freud illustrated this view by
the example of ancient Greece where the sexual drive was
considered more important than its aim: it was sexual passion that
counted and not the way in which it manifested itself (1905: 149
[7: 61]). Ten years later, in another footnote to the *Three Essays on
the Therapy of Sexuality*, Freud wrote: 'Psycho-analytic research is
most decidedly opposed to any attempt at separating off homosexuals from the rest of mankind as a group of a special character'
(1905: 145 [7: 56]). However, by suggesting that homosexuality
was due to a 'negative' solution of the Oedipus complex, Freud
contributed to this very 'separating off' of homosexuals which he
said he opposed.

Phenomenologically, the attempt to find a particular 'cause' to
explain an imprecisely defined area on the wide spectrum of
sexuality is quite meaningless. It is obvious that no single cause
could account for a spectrum of sexual behaviour that stretches
from the permanent choice of a partner of the same sex throughout life to an occasional choice, covering instances of homosexuality suggested by circumstance (as in prison or the army), as
well as a turning away from a long-time partner of the same sex to
one of the opposite sex, and vice versa. There is, of course, also
actual bisexuality for which psychoanalysis has no explanation –
except for Freud's conviction that it is the constitutional basis of
all sexuality.

For the existential psychotherapist, homosexuality is not a 'condition' brought about by specific factors, but a way of being in which whatever is 'given' is most delicately intertwined with our responses. One could say that there is no such thing as 'homosexuality' as such, rather there are infinite ways of 'being-in-the-world' homosexually. It is a way of being which can only be understood phenomenologically with a descriptive exploration of as wide a context as possible. Whether and when such an exploration is needed is, of course, a question in itself – one to which we shall return. Singling it out for exploration would imply the very thing which is here denied – that it is an extraordinary, even pathological state.

In the light of this, it is regrettable that Medard Boss, one of the few existential psychotherapists to have written on homosexuality, includes it among the 'perversions' (Boss, 1966). It needs to be said, first of all, that in the use of this term Boss does not imply dismissal or condemnation. He sees the various sexual 'perversions' as attempts to achieve loving relationships in situations where the capacity to realize them fully is inhibited or crippled. Nevertheless the 'perversions' are seen as deficiencies, and there is the implication that heterosexuality is the only sexual mode in which the potential for loving can be fully realized. A norm is set from which homosexuality deviates. An existential-phenomenological approach has no place for 'norms', as E. van Deurzen-Smith puts it: 'Existential therapists are fundamentally concerned with what matters to the client. He or she avoids making normative judgements, and renounces any ambition to, even implicitly, push the client in any particular direction' (1996: 177–8).

The reason why Boss sees heterosexuality as a norm is that only in a heterosexual union are masculine and feminine potentialities brought together. This is a surprisingly simplistic assumption. It implies that there *are* definite masculine and feminine potentialities, and that we know how to define them. Also it takes for granted that whatever is called 'masculine' is present only in men, and what is called 'feminine' is present only in women. This assumption seems to me to be neither phenomenological nor existential.

From what we have seen it seems clear that homosexuality, as such, is neither a developmental arrest that needs to be unfrozen nor a psychological disorder that needs to be alleviated or 'cured'.

Homosexual people, however, have difficulties like anybody else, and some of their difficulties may concern their sexuality – as do some of the difficulties of heterosexual people. Homosexual people are, of course, especially vulnerable in a situation in which they are targets of persecution. In this case an existential therapist will explore the context of their sexuality, as she or he would whenever there are sexual difficulties.

ILLUSTRATION

Rod came to see me because he is gay and wishes to marry and have a family. He has tried to have sexual relations with women but did not succeed. He had read that homosexuality was due to childhood events, and that their exploration might lead a homosexual person to become heterosexual. Rod had no permanent partner, and though he enjoyed frequent sexual encounters he found his loneliness intolerable.

I went along with his wish to explore his childhood and we found that he was smothered by a powerful mother while his father played only a small part in his life. This is, of course, the childhood situation seen by many therapists as giving rise to a boy's identification with mother rather than father and preparing the way for homosexual behaviour. These therapists tend to forget how often we find dominating mothers and absent fathers in the childhood of heterosexual clients!

Rod made a few more unsuccessful attempts to relate sexually to women, and eventually the theme of our talks shifted from relating sexually to relating as such. It seemed that he had always been a loner, distrustful of other people, very uncertain of what he had to offer, and therefore afraid of being cheated and exploited. Gradually he came to see that his isolation had nothing to do with his sexual choice, but that it was a protective barrier which he was afraid to dismantle. He had constructed this barrier as a defensive response to a number of threatening 'givens' among which his dominating mother and indifferent father certainly played a part. Eventually he risked a breach in this barrier and has now been living for some time with another man – a new development in his life.

Perversions

To understand the psychoanalytic approach to perversions we need to take a brief look at Freud's theory of drives. Freud distinguishes between the source, the aim and the object. The source is a bodily stimulus, the aim is the release of the tension which stimulation – once it has reached a certain degree which Freud calls 'pressure' – has built up, and the object is the means by which this tension is discharged. In the case of the sexual drive, the source is the excitation of certain bodily areas (not necessarily the genitals) including 'the production of sexual excitation by rhythmic mechanical agitation of the body' (Freud, 1905: 201 [7: 120]). When discussing infantile sexuality Freud, interestingly, also mentions 'affective processes' as sources of excitation. He says 'that all comparatively intense affective processes, including even terrifying ones, trench upon sexuality' (1905: 203 [7: 123]) – a comment that raises the difficult question of the connection between terror and sexuality which transcends mere biology. The aim of the sexual drive is often the same as the source – mouth, anus, genitals (the 'erotogenic zones'). In the adult, however, it is said to be the union with a person of the opposite sex with which the earlier objects ('component drives') have merged.

This is the point where Freud's belief in the biological existence of a variety of possible 'objects' has given way to the 'normality' of one embodied in heterosexuality. Thus, in *The Language of Psychoanalysis*, Laplanche and Pontalis characterize 'perversions' as a 'deviation from the "normal" sexual act when this is defined as coitus with a person of the opposite sex directed towards the achievement of orgasm by means of genital penetration' (Laplanche and Pontalis, 1973: 306). They continue with a summary which distinguishes three kinds of perversion:

1   orgasm is reached with other sexual objects: homosexuality (which Freud originally called 'inversion'), paedophilia, bestiality;
2   orgasm is reached through other regions of the body, for example the anus;
3   orgasm is possible only when certain extrinsic conditions are present: fetishism, transvestism, voyeurism, exhibitionism, sado-masochism. At times these conditions can, by themselves, bring about sexual release.

It is important to note that we do not talk about 'perversions' in children. As Freud sees it, children are naturally 'polymorphously perverse' (Freud, 1905: 191 [7: 109]). Thus it becomes questionable to talk of perversions as 'unnatural'. Also, most of the various types of behaviour called perverse are found as part of so-called 'normal' heterosexuality and are called perversions only when they become predominant.

In a famous saying Freud called neuroses *the negative of perversions* (1905: 165 [7: 80]). Neurotic symptoms are the result of a repression of the wishes that perversions express freely. But this non-judgemental openness is undermined by the concept of development: if heterosexuality is the aim, then the return to earlier stages is inevitably a regression. 'Development' literally means 'unfolding' and implies the emergence of something new from what is already there. It has acquired the meaning of a move from a less to a more desirable and 'mature' stage and thus gives rise to criteria of normality. Phenomenologically the butterfly is different from but not superior to the caterpillar.

Existential-phenomenologically there cannot be a process like regression, as this implies a linear view of time. If the past is always an aspect of our present experiential capacity, there is no need to 'go back' to it. The reappearance of strands of infantile sexuality in adult sexual behaviour is not surprising. In the light of the simultaneity of temporal modes, it seems unnecessary to separate 'earlier' from 'later' components.

Problems can arise when clients feel that a desired sexual activity becomes difficult or impossible. Clients may feel that masturbation takes the place of sexual relations with others, or that orgasm is dependent on wearing certain kinds of clothes. Such activities become problematic for clients because they feel they are 'not normal' by the rules of their sociocultural context – even though they are in fact quite happy with the way they experience sexual satisfaction. But it can also be that they would prefer a different way of sexual activity which appears to them more meaningful. Such clients will go to a therapist for help, and the existential therapist will explore with them the different aspects of their sexuality and their feelings about it. The important point is that it is they who are dissatisfied, and not the therapist who judges them to be 'immature' or 'inadequate' and in need of being 'sorted out'.

ILLUSTRATION

Tim was only sexually aroused when the woman he wanted to make love to wore leather gloves. Without them Tim was impotent. Leather gloves were his 'fetish' – the magical object that gave him the capacity to be sexually active. In fact, the mere presence of leather gloves, even without a woman, could bring about sexual arousal.

Psychoanalytically, the fetish represents the mother's lacking penis: the boy has never accepted its lack because it conjures up the threat of castration (Freud, 1927: 147–57 [7: 351 ff.]). This is a complicated and, in my view, rather far-fetched explanation. A more behaviouristic approach would link the leather gloves with early sexual experiences involving such gloves in one way or another.

An exploration of his relations with women showed that he had on the whole avoided sexual contact with them, and had been fully potent even with the help of his fetish on only a few occasions. He felt he had to keep women at bay – he craved for their care but feared their power. There were a number of powerful but unstable women in his family, including his mother whom he rarely saw. At the same time such women had had a magnetic attraction for him throughout his life. The development of the experiential pattern which led to his 'fetishism' never became clear. He came to see that he both needed women and was afraid of them. His 'fetish' regulated, so to speak, his relation to them. This eased his mind considerably, though we never discovered the origin of his sexual behaviour.

Sexuality and violence

The consideration of perversion brings us to the difficult question of sexual acts which involve the violation of others. This covers a wide spectrum of behaviour, from imposing the view of genitals on an unprepared spectator to child abuse, rape and sexual murder. The question of consent is, of course, fundamental though by no means always clear in actual situations. In sado-masochistic acts the claim of consent can be a controversial issue. Most people would agree that the sexual use of children is always a violation whether they 'consent' to it or not.

We are facing the central problem of the nature of human destructiveness. This is a contentious and many-layered area, and within the framework of this book my considerations are bound to be sketchy. Erich Fromm, in his *Anatomy of Human Destructiveness* (1974), gives a lucid and comprehensive account of many of the relevant issues. In an interesting exposition of Freud's 'theory of aggressiveness and destructiveness', Fromm explores an earlier view where destructiveness is seen as a component of the sexual instinct and at the same time as independent of it. In his earlier writings, Fromm points out, Freud talks about the aggressive side of the sexual drive as manifesting itself as the wish for incorporation and mastery of the loved object. But at the same time Freud proposes 'aggressiveness as being independent from the sexual instinct, as a quality of the ego instincts which oppose and hate the intrusion of outside stimuli and obstacles to the satisfaction of sexual needs and those for self-preservation' (Fromm, 1974: 584).

In 1920, Freud's *Beyond the Pleasure Principle* replaced the old dichotomy between sexual and ego instincts with a new one – that of libido (which he also called 'Eros') and the death instinct. Fromm quotes Freud's explanation of this new duality: 'besides the instinct to preserve living substance and to join it into ever larger units, there must exist another, contrary instinct seeking to dissolve those units and to bring them back to their primaeval, inorganic state. That is to say, as well as Eros there was an instinct of death' (1974: 585–6; Freud, 1930: 118–19 [12: 309–10]).

Originally the 'death instinct' seemed to be the origin of self-destructiveness but eventually Freud saw destructiveness, as such, as the death instinct turned outwards. Fromm shows clearly that the original meaning of the death instinct does not, in fact, lend itself to such a transformation. He asks: 'is there any evidence or even reason for this identity of the tendency to cessation of all excitation and the impulse to destroy?' Fromm does not think so and insists rightly, I think, that 'life's inherent tendency for slowing down and eventually to die' has nothing to do with 'the active impulse to destroy' (1974: 599). Most psychoanalysts did not accept Freud's concept of a death instinct. But, as Fromm says, 'they transformed the death instinct into a "destructive instinct" opposite to the old sexual instinct. They thus combined their loyalty to Freud with their inability to go beyond the old-fashioned instinct-theory' (1974: 601). This polarization of instincts still governs a great deal of psychoanalytic theory and its understanding of the connection between violence and sexuality.

Fromm's position is different. He believes that in man 'instinctive determination has reached its maximum decrease' (1974:

301). In other words, our responses are only to a small extent instinctively determined: 'Man's irrationality is caused by the fact that he lacks instincts, and not by their presence' (1974: 353). Human destructiveness is the result of a choice. In an approach that comes at times quite near to that of existential phenomenology, Fromm sees destructiveness as 'one of the possible answers to psychic needs that are rooted in the existence of man' (1974: 294). He says that 'the need for relatedness can be answered by love and kindness – or by dependence, sadism, masochism, destructiveness' (1974: 340). The existential phenomenologist would describe relatedness not as an existential need but as an existential 'given', to which there can be loving or destructive responses.

The important view which Fromm and the existential phenomenologist share is that destructiveness is not an aspect of sexuality itself. Fromm distinguishes 'benign' from 'malignant' aggression. Benign aggression is the ability to move 'forwards towards a goal without undue hesitation, doubt or fear' (1974: 256). This is the original meaning of the Latin verb '*aggredi*'. Some people see this moving forward as an inevitable component of a sexual approach. But this form of 'aggression' would be considered benign by Fromm: its aim is not to overpower or destroy. (The Latin word is intransitive!) The various forms of sadism illustrate what Fromm calls 'malignant' aggression. Freud came to see sadism as a blending of Eros and the death instinct turned outward towards others. Fromm rejects such an instinctual interpretation and asserts that the core of all manifestations of sadism is 'the passion to have absolute and unrestricted control over a living being' (1974: 384). Fromm sees this 'passion' as rooted in the very 'limitations of human existence' – sadism being the 'transformation of impotence into the illusion of omnipotence' (1974: 386). Life's uncertainty and unpredictability can give rise to feelings of anxiety and powerlessness. A possible response is a compulsive search for absolute power, manifesting itself in the wide-ranging spectrum of sadistic practices.

Once destructiveness is no longer seen as an aspect of sexuality itself, it is possible to distinguish between a sexual and a non-sexual sadism. Sexuality is one of the intrinsic aspects of our 'Being-in-the-world', and as such can become one of the ways in which it can affirm or destroy existence.

Summing up Fromm's arguments and emphasizing their existential-phenomenological relevance, we can say the following about the relation between sexuality and violence:

(a) Violence is not an aspect of sexuality itself which has made itself independent of its context.
(b) Rather sexuality can be the potential channel which carries a destructive response to existential 'givens'.
(c) One of these 'givens' can be relatedness itself – which can become the target of rejection, distortion and destruction.
(d) Another 'given' is life's uncertainty and unpredictability which can lead to feelings of panic and powerlessness. These in turn may give rise to the compulsive need to overpower and destroy others sexually.

An existential phenomenologist may wish to add: if 'Being-in-the-world' is always 'being-with-others', and existential relatedness is the mutual openness of human beings to each other, the sexual violation of the other deprives him or her of their subjectivity, turning them into objects, and there is a destruction of existence itself.

References

Boss, M. (1966) *Sinn und Gehalt der Sexuellen Perversionen*. 3rd edn. Bern: Huber.

Deurzen-Smith, E. van (1996) 'Existential therapy', in W. Dryden (ed.), *Handbook of Individual Therapy*. London: Sage Publications.

Freud, S. (1905) *Three Essays on the Theory of Sexuality*. S.E. VII. London: Hogarth Press. (Pelican Freud Library. Vol. 7. Harmondsworth: Penguin Books.)

Freud, S. (1920) *Beyond the Pleasure Principle*. S.E. XVIII. London: Hogarth Press. (Pelican Freud Library. Vol. 11. Harmondsworth: Penguin Books.)

Freud, S. (1923) *The Ego and the Super-Ego*. S.E. XIX. London: Hogarth Press. (Pelican Freud Library. Vol. 11. Harmondsworth: Penguin Books.)

Freud, S. (1924) *The Dissolution of the Oedipus Complex*. S.E. XIX. London: Hogarth Press. (Pelican Freud Library. Vol. 7. Harmondsworth: Penguin Books.)

Freud, S. (1925) *Some Psychical Consequences of the Anatomical Distinction between the Sexes.* S.E. XIX. London: Hogarth Press. (Pelican Freud Library. Vol. 7. Harmondsworth: Penguin Books.)

Freud, S. (1926) *The Question of Lay Analysis.* S.E. XX. London: Hogarth Press.

Freud, S. (1927) *Fetishism.* S.E. XXI. London: Hogarth Press. (Pelican Freud Library. Vol. 7. Harmondsworth: Penguin Books.)

Freud, S. (1930) *Civilization and its Discontents.* S.E. XXI. London: Hogarth Press. (Pelican Freud Library. Vol. 12. Harmondsworth: Penguin Books.)

Fromm, E. (1974) *The Anatomy of Human Destructiveness.* Harmondsworth: Penguin Books.

Jones, E. (1961) *The Life and Work of Sigmund Freud.* Ed. and abr. L. Trilling and S. Marcus. Harmondsworth: Penguin Books.

Laplanche, L. and Pontalis, J.B. (1973) *The Language of Psychoanalysis.* London: Karnac Books.

Madison, G.B. (1981) *The Phenomenology of Merleau-Ponty.* Athens, OH: Ohio University Press.

Merleau-Ponty, M. (1962) *Phenomenology of Perception.* Tr. C. Smith. London: Routledge & Kegan Paul.

Sartre, J.P. (1958) *Being and Nothingness.* Tr. H. Barnes. New York: Philosophical Library.

11
Withdrawal and Delusion

Withdrawal and delusion are two moves in our relation to reality which in extreme situations may manifest themselves as 'psychotic' disturbances. We may withdraw from a reality we cannot master, and we may replace it by one we have created ourselves. It is questionable whether a clear distinction between neurosis and psychosis can in fact be made or what the criteria for such a distinction could be. Opinions on this vary widely among different theorists and therapists. Not many psychotherapists have the opportunity to see people diagnosed as 'psychotic'. However, in any therapeutic situation phenomena which may be called psychotic could emerge. These need to be recognized and understood, if only in order to suggest some additional or alternative help if this is necessary.

The psychoanalytic approach

Freud did make a definite distinction between neurosis and psychosis. In one of his two papers on this question he says: *'neurosis is the result of a conflict between the ego and its id, whereas psychosis is the analogous outcome of a similar disturbance in the relations between the ego and the external world'* (Freud, 1924a: 149 [10: 213]). Later in the same paper, Freud adds another category to the distinction between psychosis and neurosis – that of the 'narcissistic psychoneuroses'. These are based on a conflict between ego and super-ego, and he includes melancholia among them: 'we find reasons for separating states like melancholia from the other psychoses' (1924a: 152 [10: 216]). It is noticeable that Freud uses the word 'melancholia' – according to Rycroft an 'obsolescent term for what is now called depression (particularly endogenous depression, depressive illness or the depressive phase of manic-depressive psychosis' (Rycroft, 1995: 101). The existential therapists, as we shall see, also prefer this term to 'depression', which is now so widely used that it is almost meaningless.

In his second paper on the question, Freud is concerned with what neurosis and psychosis have in common: 'in neurosis a piece of reality is avoided by a sort of flight, whereas in psychosis it is remodelled' (Freud, 1924b: 185, [10: 223]). There is here an indication that, in spite of their difference, neurosis and psychosis have a common ground in their avoidance of reality and we may feel justified to infer that this can, to some extent, blur the distinction.

Freud did not believe that psychoanalytic therapy could reach psychosis. This conviction was rooted in his theoretical assumptions. Anna Freud sums up the reasons why Freud thought psychotic patients unsuitable for psychoanalytic psychotherapy: they lacked 'a more or less normal ego that has retained the capacity for reality testing, self-observation, and insight into illness; the libidinal cathexis of real persons which makes the emotional transference to the analyst possible; the readiness of the inner world to perceive, acknowledge, and at least partially subject itself to external influences' (Freud, 1986: 560). We shall return to this characterization at a later point when we discuss an existential perspective on psychotic disturbance.

Some post-Freudian psychoanalysts do not share Freud's pessimism with regard to a psychoanalytic approach to psychotic phenomena. But they admit that it is necessary to modify psychoanalytic practice in order to establish a contact with their patients. They think that transferences do in fact develop which are often quite intense and need to be handled with great care as they may represent the first attempt of the patient to form a relationship with another person. A number of psychoanalysts propose also a dispositional factor, perhaps of a biological nature. And in some cases a combination of psychotherapy and medication is recommended. There seems to be a general agreement that an orthodox psychoanalytic approach is unable to explain the psychotic patient's situation or to break through to his or her distress.

The important exception to this view is the approach of the Kleinian school. Their firm belief in the psychoanalytic explanation and treatment of psychoses is based on their characteristic conceptualization of an intrapsychic space in which destructive impulses dominate from early childhood onwards. These impulses are seen as innate, as manifestations of Freud's concept of the death instinct. Freud himself said of the death instinct that: 'The instinctual forces which seek to conduct life into death may also be operating in protozoa from the first, and yet their effects may be so completely concealed by the life-preserving forces that it may be very hard to find any direct evidence of their presence' (Freud, 1920: 49 [11: 321-2]). Melanie Klein had a radically different view. Direct evidence of the presence of the death instinct emerged in the form of destructive impulses, and she saw psychotic behaviour essentially as a defence against these. The purpose of such defences was to ward off the overwhelming anxiety which the destructive impulses generated. Hinshelwood gives a vivid description of these defence mechanisms. They 'include splitting, denial, idealization, projection, introjection and identification. They are mostly suffused with omnipotence and carried out with great violence in phantasy' (Hinshelwood, 1989: 393).

It needs to be added here that Melanie Klein believed in 'psychotic phases' in childhood development, and she saw these as 'fixation points' for psychotic illness.

This is not the place to give an adequate overview of Kleinian assumptions; Robert Hinshelwood's *Dictionary of Kleinian Thought* (1989) provides a lucid introduction to this complex Kleinian framework. In the present context it is important to note that here is a theory of psychosis that is entirely intra-psychic, does not refer to reality in the way that Freud did and also differs from Freud in the belief that the psychotic patient can be therapeutically reached by a strictly psychoanalytic approach. There is - as in all Kleinian analysis - a special emphasis on transference. Kleinians believe that there is always a 'sane' part of the person which can be reached. In other words, for the Kleinian analyst there is no clear-cut distinction between neurosis and psychosis; the same fundamental dynamics are seen to underlie them both.

A few words need to be added on the so-called 'borderline' disorders. Definitions of this condition vary widely, and the usefulness of the term which covers a wide spectrum of neurotic and psychotic characteristics has been questioned. A recent overview of contemporary psychoanalytic practice has this to say: "The DSM III-R descriptive criteria for a diagnosis of Borderline Personality Disorder (BPD) can be summarized as "stable instability" comprising: intense but unstable personal relationships; self-destructiveness; constant efforts to avoid real and imagined abandonment; chronic dysphoria such as anger or boredom; transient psychotic episodes or cognitive distortions; impulsivity; poor social adaptation; and identity disturbance' (Bateman and Holmes, 1995: 223). Once again, a clear-cut distinction between neurosis and psychosis seems to be put into question.

The existential-phenomenological approach

Looking again at Anna Freud's summary of her father's reasons for declaring psychotic patients 'unsuitable' for psychoanalytic therapy, we find three basic obstacles: (a) the ego is damaged and incapable of telling what is real from what is not; (b) no emotional contact with other people is possible; (c) the inner world of the 'psychotic' can neither perceive the external world nor adapt to it.

Considering these obstacles may help us to understand the radically different way in which the existential phenomenologist sees the psychologically disturbed person's relation to the world. First, the existential phenomenologist does not assume the existence of a structured 'psyche' within a person, one part of which – for instance the ego – can be impaired and thus prevent the whole from functioning properly. Existence is 'Being-in-the-world': it is always a person's relation to the world that may be damaged, it is the a priori interaction between *Dasein* and what it meets and addresses that may be disturbed.

Second, if relatedness as such is a 'given', if the world is essentially a 'with-world' (Heidegger), the contact with others is always there though it may be distorted or crippled – this is the meaning of intersubjectivity. Therefore what psychoanalysts call 'transference' is never lacking, we never cease responding to each other in one way or another.

Third, there is no distinction between an inner and outer world. There is one world in which I, among others, have a place.

Our experiences of this world do, of course, differ as do our personal histories, but there is always the openness of a common ground.

Thus Freud's questions about the openness of 'psychotic' clients to therapy do not arise – the philosophical framework within which existential therapists try to understand their disturbances applies to 'psychotic' clients as much as it does to other clients. Of course, this does not mean that the therapeutic situation is the same: this always depends on what the client brings into it and how the therapist responds.

As we have seen, varying approaches to psychological disturbances can be found within the wider existential-phenomenological framework. In Chapter 2 we touched on the different ways in which Ludwig Binswanger and Medard Boss interpret Heidegger's thinking of Being as Being-in-the-world (pp. 16–19). This distinction shows particularly clearly in their approaches to the so-called psychotic disorders.

Binswanger's approach

Binswanger proposes that each person constitutes his or her own world, has a specific 'world design' which is, however, not a response to particular life events but is a priori, 'transcendental' – a part of the very structure of his or her being. The traumatic experience which psychoanalysis sees as the origin of the disturbance already presupposes, in Binswanger's view, a certain 'world-design'. This 'existential a priori', as it is also called, runs like a theme through all the various manifestations of a person's life, and the therapist's task is the exploration and clarification of these themes.

In the case of schizophrenia – both Binswanger and Boss adhere to the usual diagnostic classification – the theme is that 'of a break-down in the consistency of natural experience' (Binswanger, 1963: 252). The consistency of natural experience – its disorder, its gaps – cannot be tolerated. The experienced fragmentation of life is fought in different ways – there is an 'inability to "let things be". Everywhere we encounter this unquenchable longing to re-establish the disturbed order, to fill the gaps in

experience with ever new ideas, activities, undertakings, distractions, obligations, and ideals' (Binswanger, 1963: 253).
The way of 'ordering' the disordered experience is to split it into alternatives. On the one hand, an ideal position is pursued which is 'extravagant' (Needleman's translation of the German '*verstiegen*' which literally means the state of having 'climbed' into a position from which we can neither ascend nor descend) and unmaintainable. On the other hand, the opposite ideal exerts a powerful attraction as well. Milder forms of such a split are, of course, familiar. The need for absolute security can be paired with the pursuit of reckless adventure, or the ideal of sexual purity with the temptation of sexual excess. In extreme cases, 'Dasein is torn by the struggle between both aspects of the alternatives into which it is split' (Binswanger, 1963: 255). One way of dealing with this ambivalence is the tortuous concealment of whatever undermines the ideal.

The only way out of this destructive impasse may be 'a resignation or a renunciation of the whole antinomic problem as such, and that takes the form of an existential retreat' (Binswanger, 1963: 258). This 'retreat' leads either to suicide or to insanity. Binswanger presents suicide as 'the freest decision of which the Dasein has been able to avail itself' (1963: 258). By comparison, insanity is the least free way out; 'What is renounced is life as an independent, autonomous selfhood. The Dasein . . . surrenders itself over to existential powers alien to itself. What we have here is a particularly radical capitulation of the Dasein' (1963: 259).

The other psychiatrically diagnosed psychotic condition is the 'bipolar' manic-depressive disorder. This Binswanger conceives as rooted in a breakdown of the experience of time. This is once again an a priori world design running as a theme through the patient's life. In the case of melancholia (Binswanger does not speak of 'depression' which he considers to be a vague term with too many meanings), the theme is a clinging to the past taking the form of guilt mixed with fear of the future manifesting itself as the certainty of punishment. In this blend of past and future the present has no place. Everything that is possible has already happened. Life is ruled by the shadow of loss – a loss which is not just anticipated but is already fact.

On the other hand, the manic experience knows neither past nor future. It is a mere present, based on nothing and without direction. It is characterized by 'volatility and a fuzzy view of an undefined world' and there is an 'impression of floating, skipping and leaping when we turn . . . to the verbal expressions of these patients and their world of thought' (Binswanger, 1955: 255 – my translation).

Again, this particular psychological disorder is, in Binswanger's view, not brought about by a life event. A particular trauma could not have resulted in this disturbance if the specific world design – the break-up of the experience of temporality – had been absent. Therefore Binswanger does not distinguish between reactive and endogenous melancholia: 'the so-called reactive melancholia, if it is truly melancholia, is endogenous, a phase of manic-depressive psychosis' (Binswanger, 1960: 19–20 – my translation). The relation between the two poles of this disorder was seen by Binswanger in 1945 as an 'intensification and elaboration . . . of the universal enmeshment of death in life, and life in death' (Binswanger, 1955: 259 – my translation). In 1960, under the increasing influence of Husserl's 'transcendental' phenomenology, the link between melancholia and mania is the a priori 'world design' – the break-up of the experience of time's continuous flow.

Binswanger's theoretical assumptions are illustrated throughout his extensive work by detailed studies of patients' histories which are rich in stimulating phenomenological observations and insights. However, with regard to a psychotherapeutic approach to these patients, a difficulty arises to which Holzhey-Kunz has drawn attention (Holzhey-Kunz, 1994: 24). If the 'world design' is transcendental and thus must be thought of as a presupposition underlying the way of the patients' being-in-the-world, it seems beyond change. Therapy can then only clarify and help the patient to understand how things are; and we know that this can often be helpful. Binswanger, however, seems to have had more than this in mind.

At the end of his paper on 'Extravagance', Binswanger says:

What we call psychotherapy is basically no more than an attempt to bring the patient to a point where he can 'see' the manner in which the totality of human experience of 'being-in-the-world' is structured and to see at which of its junctures he has overreached himself. That is: the goal of psychotherapy is to bring the patient safely back 'down to earth' from his Extravagance. Only from this point is any new departure and ascent possible. (Binswanger, 1963: 348–9)

But what does he mean by 'new departure' when our being is structured by a world-design that is independent of any life event?

Boss's approach

Boss's understanding of psychotic phenomena is informed by Heidegger's concept of 'Being-in-the-world'. This is not the world constituted by a person's specific world-design but by the world in which we all participate, standing out ('ex-sisting') into its openness, perceiving and responding to what shows itself.

Schizophrenia, in Boss's view, 'must be seen as a disturbance of the specific being-in-the-world which is the nature of human being'. This Being-in-the-world 'is the carrying, sustaining, maintaining, and holding open of a clear worldly realm of perception and responsiveness that all people carry out, though each in his own individual way' (Boss, 1994: 235). People called 'schizophrenic' suffer in varying degrees from an impairment of this 'ability to be responsive and open to what is encountered' (Boss, 1994: 235). This shows itself in a narrowing down of what they can perceive and at the same time in a crippling of their responses. But it can also show itself in a tendency to be overwhelmed by what they encounter so that they feel 'at the beck and call of everything and everyone' (Boss, 1994: 226). One way of dealing with the overpowering demands of the world is to submit to them.

In an untranslated lecture (1979: 347 ff.) Boss brings his existential-phenomenological understanding to bear on the phenomena of hallucination and delusion. In an untranslatable word-play he sees both the 'erecting of barriers' (*Beschränkung*) and the 'dismantling of barriers' (*Entschränkung*) as aspects of the disturbed capacity to respond to the addresses of the world. While the one leads to withdrawal from the relational context, the other leads to the disappearance of a 'protective filter': demands and threats come so close and grow so powerful that they are experienced as present and concrete (*Vergegenwärtigung*) – as voices, hallucinations and delusions.

Boss sees both manic and melancholic states as an impairment of the capacity to 'stand out' into the openness of the world. In the manic state, patients: 'cannot maintain what they encounter in space and time where it is nor let it come into being as what it has to be. The perception of these patients is so severely restricted that in each thing they encounter they see nothing but a single significance: everything addresses them only as something to be seized and gobbled up' (Boss, 1994: 218). We could say that these patients have fallen out of context and have lost all sense of the totality of their situation. As Binswanger also stresses, the flow of temporality is disrupted; there is nothing but a disconnected present.

In the melancholic state patients 'see only themselves, and the world around them only as far as it is directly related to them in a particular way. But while the manic sees himself as an omnipotent godlike creature . . . the melancholic sees in himself nothing but emptiness, worthlessness and culpability' (Boss, 1994: 219). The openness of the world has shrunk to one and one context only: failure, guilt and punishment. The multidimensionality of time has been reduced to the past, which is imprisoning the future and has destroyed the present. This deformation of temporality is also described by Binswanger.

Boss introduces here the notion of existential guilt. Whatever reasons melancholics may find for their feelings of failure and guilt, they are in fact indebted to their own unrealized potentialities. Heidegger's concept of authenticity ascribes to us the capacity to free ourselves from the imprisonment by '*das Man*' ('the they') and to find our own responses to what we encounter. When we fail to do this, we experience guilt which is part of our humanity.

Holzhey-Kunz (1994) stresses the difference between the approaches of Binswanger and Boss. Both propose the presence of constitutional elements in the genesis of psychotic behaviour. But Binswanger's 'world-design' is a priori and covers 'abnormal' as well as normal attitudes: it seems inaccessible to change, as we have seen, and thus poses questions for the practice of psychotherapy. Boss, on the other hand, believes that each of us has innate possibilities of responding to the world, though these may be different for different people; and that life events, particularly inadequate upbringing, can undermine and distort those responses. This opens up possibilities for change – and thus for therapeutic practice.

Comments on therapy

1 The existential-phenomenological approach to 'psychotic' states – as to any other form of psychological disturbance – is not to assume an imbalance within an intrapsychic system but to explore the impairment of the client's human capacity to respond to his or her specific world as well as to the intrinsic aspects of Being-in-the-world as such. Here conflicts within the field of relatedness or intersubjectivity are of special importance.

2 Thus a clear-cut distinction between 'psychotic' and 'neurotic' disorders cannot be made. We have already seen how, in the so-called 'borderline' disorders, 'neurotic' and 'psychotic' traits can either be found side by side or blending into each other. The more radical the denial of reality (the 'given') is, the more fundamental will be the withdrawal from it or its replacement by delusion, a kind of anti-reality.

3 The existential therapist will try to help the client to clarify his or her total situation, exploring the world he or she has created, focusing on the important 'themes' as they emerge without necessarily seeing them as 'a priori' and thus beyond change. This would be the 'ontic' aspect of the therapy, echoing to some extent Binswanger's approach.

4 The existential therapist would also try to help the client to discover where he or she is in conflict with unavoidable dimensions of Being as such, for instance with the inevitability of death, choice, relatedness. This would be the 'ontological' aspect of the therapy, suggested by Boss's daseinsanalytic perspective. I do not think that Binswanger's and Boss's approaches necessarily exclude each other.

5 It is, of course, clear that the more radical the rejection of reality turns out to be, the more difficult it will be to help the client to comprehend his or her total situation. It may be even more difficult to help the client to find a new and more

fruitful response to the reality she or he has rejected. But it is necessary to envisage change within the realm of possibility though it may frequently be only a potentiality.

ILLUSTRATION 1

Binswanger reports 'the case of a young girl who at the age of five experienced a puzzling attack of anxiety and fainting when her heel got stuck in her skate and separated from her shoe' (May et al., 1958: 202–3). The girl developed a 'heel phobia' from then on which lasted into adulthood – her heels had to be nailed to her soles, and nobody was allowed to touch her heels or even mention heels. Heels had become the trigger of an overwhelming anxiety.

Psychoanalysis would see this phobia as a form of 'separation anxiety' leading back to the trauma of being separated from mother at the time of birth. Binswanger does not exclude this possibility as a contributing factor, but adds: 'Each of us has experienced the "birth trauma" but some lose their heels without developing an hysterical phobia' (May et al., 1958: 203). Binswanger assumes that the girl's 'world-design' 'is the category of continuity, of continuous connection and containment' (May et al., 1958: 203). This world-design is not the result of losing the heel, it is 'a priori' and becomes manifest through this particular incident. The 'theme' of this girl's being-in-the-world is a fear of what is new, unexpected and discontinuous.

According to Boss, Heidegger used Binswanger's report of this particular example of phobia in order to criticize the notion of a world-design. He accuses Binswanger of 'turning existence into a formula and emptying it of all factual content' (Heidegger, 1987: 257 – my translation); the particular phenomenon – it is a heel she loses and not, say, a glove – is too quickly left behind and subordinated to an all-embracing concept.

Binswanger does not tell us anything about a therapeutic approach to this girl's phobia. It seems to me that her concern for continuity and her fear of separation could be seen as a denial of the ontological 'givens' of our 'thrownness' and the limitation of our existence. I do not think we are committed to think of her concerns and fears as 'transcendental' and unchangeable. They may be open to therapeutic clarification.

ILLUSTRATION 2

Boss introduces a young man who 'complained that he had always felt himself at the beck and call of everything and everyone he encountered. His slavish submission to the appealing, inviting, challenging character of whatever was present in his experience gradually became grotesque so that, for instance, a chair could compel him to sit on it just because it was there to be sat on' (Boss, 1994: 226).

Boss understands this behaviour as a disturbance of the capacity of this man to meet the world in openness, freely responding to it. Rather he had to submit to its demands. This was particularly striking in his relation to people. 'If our young man encountered a gardener at work, he felt so emotionally swallowed up by him that he had to do exactly what the gardener did, and through him, become a gardener' (1994: 227). Boss's understanding takes into account the young man's history. His parents had said that their son might be able to be a gardener – and this again was a power to which he had to submit: 'their thought was their command' (1994: 227). There is an imbalance of power, not within the patient's 'psyche' but in his relation to the world.

The young man was in therapy for eight years and 'the therapist was able to arrest the illness from further progression, to preserve the patient from slipping into confusion, and to bring the patient gradually to recognition of the world which, until then, he had blindly obeyed' (1994: 226). Binswanger's prediction of a 'new departure' which was difficult to reconcile with his concept of an 'a priori' world-design seems a realistic possibility in the case of Boss's young man.

References

Bateman, A. and Holmes, J. (1995) Introduction to Psychoanalysis. Contemporary Theory and Practice. London: Routledge.

Binswanger, L. (1955) Ausgewählte Vorträge und Aufsätze. Band II. Bern: Francke Verlag.

Binswanger, L. (1960) Melancholie und Manie. Phenomenologische Studien. Pfullingen: Neske.

Binswanger, L. (1963) Being-in-the-World. Selected Papers. Tr. J. Needleman. New York: Basic Books

Boss, M. (1979) Von der Psychoanalyse zur Daseinsanalyse. Wien: Europa Verlag.

Boss, M. (1994) Existential Foundations of Medicine and Psychology. Northvale, NJ: Jason Aronson.

Freud, S. (1920) Beyond the Pleasure Principle. S.E. XVIII. London: Hogarth Press. (Pelican Freud Library. Vol. 11. Harmondsworth: Penguin Books.)

Freud, S. (1924a) Neurosis and Psychosis. S.E. XIX. London: Hogarth Press. (Pelican Freud Library. Vol. 10. Harmondsworth: Penguin Books.)

Freud, S. (1924b) The Loss of Reality in Neurosis and Psychosis. S.E. XIX. London: Hogarth Press. (Pelican Freud Library. Vol. 10. Harmondsworth: Penguin Books.)

Freud, S. (1986) The Essentials of Psychoanalysis. Ed. Anna Freud. Harmondsworth: Penguin Books.

Heidegger, M. (1987) *Zollikoner Seminare. Protokolle – Gespräche – Briefe.* Ed. Medard Boss. Frankfurt a.M.: Klostermann.

Hinshelwood, R.D. (1989) *A Dictionary of Kleinian Thought.* London: Free Association Books.

Holzhey-Kunz, A. (1994) *Leiden am Dasein.* Wien: Passagen Verlag.

May, R., Angel, E. and Ellenberger, H.F. (eds) (1958) *Existence.* New York: Basic Books.

Rycroft, C. (1995) *A Critical Dictionary of Psychoanalysis.* 2nd edn. Harmondsworth: Penguin Books.

12

Aims of Psychotherapy

It has never been easy to formulate the aims of any therapeutic process. Inevitably they will vary with the theoretical orientation of the therapist, but within a particular orientation different therapists may describe their aims differently. Aims depend also on the expectations and personalities of the clients. They may also change in the course of a particular therapy. Some therapists will insist that they have no specific therapeutic aims. However, I think that certain broad directions can be distinguished and that they are to some extent determined by the chosen theoretical model.

Being aware of the inevitable oversimplification, I propose the following distinction of therapeutic aims: (a) the removal of symptoms; (b) a change in the intrapsychic structure; (c) the facing and reintegration of an unaccepted or unacceptable aspect of life. I will discuss these three types of aim, comparing as before the therapeutic positions of psychoanalysis and existential psychotherapy.

The removal of symptoms

Both psychoanalysis and existential psychotherapy would agree that the mere removal of symptoms – which is the main concern of the behavioural therapies – is insufficient. At the same time their evaluation of symptoms differs.

For the psychoanalytic therapist the symptom is a 'compromise between the repressed wish and the dictates of the repressing agency' (Rycroft, 1995: 181). The task of the therapist is to dismantle this compromise by discovering the repressed wish, freeing it from the distorting force which presents it as a symptom, and allowing it to find its place in the client's consciousness.

Mere removal of the symptom would compel the unaccepted wish to find a different disguise and present itself as a different symptom. Thus the symptom needs to be analysed and not just removed.

The existential therapist takes the symptom more seriously. For the symptom is a phenomenon and thus an important aspect of the total situation presented by the client. Understanding its meaning and context, interpreting it hermeneutically rather than analytically, will help to clarify the total situation. If, for instance, a client suffering from compulsive hand washing spends many hours a day in an attempt to keep his or her hands free from germs, the loss of time as such and its effect on the life of the client is an important theme for therapeutic exploration. But it is only one aspect of the total situation, and the disappearance of this symptom would leave many questions unconsidered.

Change in the intrapsychic structure

Psychoanalysis presents the psyche as a structure made up of parts, the relative strengths of which determine balance or states of conflict in our mental life. Mental processes are complicated by the introduction of a separate 'unconscious' area into this structure. The important difference between this and the existential view is that here the centre of gravity lies *within* the subject.

For the existential therapist, however, all human being is 'Being-in-the-world'. The emphasis is on the a priori involvement of the subject and world, world and subject, subject and subject. Existential therapy does not try to change the hypothetical intrapsychic structure of the individual client – that is, it does not help to 'strengthen' the ego or 'weaken' the super-ego – but tries to clarify the modes of involvement, the fields of inter-subjectivity and communication. Its therapeutic space is not the 'inner world' of the client but his or her area of interaction with a world of which he or she is a part.

Here psychoanalysis and existential psychotherapy have no common ground as the existential view does not posit a psychic structure 'within' the individual.

Facing the unacceptable

Here the common ground seems clear. Most forms of psychotherapy see the non-acceptance of something which seems unacceptable, the turning-away from difficulties which cannot be mastered, the denial of aspects of life which cannot be integrated, as a source of conflict and disturbance. Thus psychoanalysis and existential therapy would initially ask a similar question: what is it the client does not want to know, cannot open up to, cannot allow to be true?

The nature of the unacceptable, however, differs, the means of keeping the unaccepted at bay are seen differently, as is the process of integration. Perhaps these differences can be represented schematically:

Psychoanalysis	*Existential therapy*
unacceptable impulse (drive, wish)	unacceptable aspects of existence ('thrownness', need to choose, death)
↓	↓
repressed into the unconscious	dropped from awareness
↓	↓
return of rejected impulses warded off by	return of rejected 'existentials' warded off by
↓	↓
symptom formation, inappropriate behaviour, disguised expression in dreams	evasion, distraction, denial

Though over-simplified, this comparison brings out, I hope, some of the important differences between the two approaches. The psychoanalytic model is essentially biological, concerned with the fate of 'drives' which when unaccepted are 'repressed' and attempt to return in disguise. The conflict is between 'conscious' and 'unconscious' forces within a person's psyche. This is imagined as a structured 'psychic apparatus', to use Freud's expression. The existential view is philosophical, seeing man as a reflecting future-directed being in conflict with some 'given' characteristics of existence. These he or she is free to accept or deny.

In the case of psychoanalysis change is seen to take place 'inside', intrapsychically, within the person; whereas in the case of existential therapy it occurs 'outside', 'in-between', at the point of our involvement with the world.

Authenticity and psychotherapy

The aim of existential psychotherapy is often described as the emergence of a more 'authentic' way of living. Let us first take a closer look at the word 'authentic' which is often inaccurately employed. It is derived from a Latin verb which originally meant 'increase, promote, originate' (*Shorter OED*). 'Authentic' itself is generally used to indicate that something is 'genuine'. A work of art, for instance, is 'authenticated' as being, in fact, what it is said to be – say, a genuine Vermeer.

The implication of this usage is that by saying that something is genuine, we employ certain criteria for distinguishing it from something that is not genuine. It is by no means easy to establish the genuineness of a work of art – the Vermeer forgeries deceived many connoisseurs – but the proof of authenticity is within reach as long as a comparison with what is known to be genuine is possible. But it is much more difficult to talk of 'authentic' actions or feelings: for what are the reliable criteria which entitle us to call an action or a feeling 'inauthentic'? When we judge somebody's friendliness to be 'false', we are talking of our own impressions, which may be influenced by many factors – not least by our own feelings.

This question haunts the distinction between a 'true' and a 'false' self, which makes its appearance in a paper by D.W. Winnicott (1965) and in R.D. Laing's book, *The Divided Self* (1960). There are important differences between Winnicott's and Laing's concepts. Laing is concerned with the phenomenological comprehension of the schizoid personality, while Winnicott explores the process of human development. But the common theme of these writers' assumptions is that there is a part of ourselves which submits to the demands of the world – the 'false self' – while another withdraws from them – the 'true self'. This submission has a fundamental consequence: it separates us from what we 'truly' are.

Winnicott stresses the ambivalent function of the false self. It is, on the one hand, the 'caretaker' of its true twin which is seen as vulnerable, unworldly and in need of a mediator who knows the ways of the world: 'Its defensive function is to hide and protect the True Self, whatever that may be' (Winnicott, 1965: 142). On the other hand, 'there is a very strong tendency for the mind to become the location of the False Self, and in this case there develops a dissociation between intellectual activity and psycho-somatic existence' (Winnicott, 1965: 144). Thus the false self can become the true self's enemy in the shape of destructive intel-lectualization.

The trouble with this psychological dualism is that it tries to divide the indivisible. Where does the false self end and the true self begin? Winnicott seems to be aware of this difficulty when he uses the epithet, 'whatever that may be' in his description of the false self's protective function. Winnicott's uncertainty also shows in his later proposition that 'it is more true to say that the False Self hides the infant's inner reality than to say that it hides the True Self' (1965: 148). Winnicott's unease with the division he had created comes out most clearly when, towards the end of his paper, the true self is described essentially as an experience: 'There is but little point in formulating a True Self idea except for the purpose of trying to understand the False Self, hence it does no more than collect together the details of the experience of aliveness' (Winnicott, 1965: 148).

Laing's description of the two selves needs to be seen in the context of his exploration of the schizoid state. The true self, which he calls the 'inner' self, is 'occupied in maintaining its identity and freedom by being transcendent, unembodied, and thus never to be grasped. . . . Its aim is to be pure subject, without any objective existence' (Laing, 1960: 94–5). It is a question of how far this self can be called 'true' as its qualities are described as defences against a threatening world. About the false self, Laing says that it 'arises in compliance with the intentions or expectations of the other, or with what is imagined to be the other's intentions or expectations' (1960: 98). This is again the description of a defence and thus the difference between these two selves is less clear-cut.

But whatever the differences of Winnicott's and Laing's presentation of a 'divided' self, they share the basic assumption that what we 'really' are is prevented from showing itself. Therapy is then the attempt to help what is true to break through the person's imprisonment by what is false.

It is R.D. Laing who, in a footnote, connects the concept of the false self with the notion of inauthenticity: 'The false self is one way of not being oneself. The following are a few of the more important studies within the existentialist tradition relevant to the understanding of the false self, as one way of living inauthentically' (1960: 94). Laing then proceeds to give a list of titles which, among others, mentions Heidegger's *Being and Time* (1962) and Sartre's discussion of 'bad faith' in *Being and Nothingness* (1958).

Sartre's concept of 'bad faith' is often seen as a characteristic of living inauthentically. It is the denial of our freedom to respond to what we meet, and thus of our responsibility. This denial expresses itself in phrases like: 'I can't help it, this is the way I am' or 'circumstances don't leave me any choice'. But it is also – and this is rarely sufficiently stressed – the denial of our 'facticity', the 'given' aspects of the world in which we find ourselves. It is in this tension between our condition as human beings and our ability to respond to it that our freedom is rooted. Betty Cannon describes this double aspect of freedom very succinctly: 'I fall into bad faith if I take one or both of the two dishonest positions about reality: If I pretend either to be free in a world without facts or to be a fact in a world without freedom' (Cannon, 1991: 46). The first of these positions could be called manic – 'there is nothing I can't do' – and the other depressive – 'there is nothing I can do'.

In her paper 'The Survival of the Self' (1996a), Emmy van Deurzen-Smith distinguishes between the self as 'process' and the self as 'essence'. The existential approach sees the self as 'a centre of gravity' which 'is altered as we enter into contact with the world' (van Deurzen-Smith, 1996a: 59). Laing's self is still the self as essence, as substance – a part of a structured psyche inside the person which can be divided into 'true' and 'false'. This is also the case with the self of Winnicott, less surprisingly since he never denied his psychoanalytic roots. It is here that the radical difference between a non-existential and an existential concept of

AIMS OF PSYCHOTHERAPY   125

authenticity can be found. From an existential point of view there
can be no authentic (true) or inauthentic (false) self, but only an
authentic way of Being-in-the-world.
Heidegger does not speak of a self when he describes (the)
human being. He speaks of *Dasein* which, in his words, 'must
always be seen as "Being-in-the-world", as the concern for things
and involvement with those who are with us, as the being with
persons we meet – never just as a subject on his or her own'
(Heidegger, 1987: 204 – my translation). 'Involvement' (*Sorge*) is
frequently translated as 'care' but I feel involvement is prefer-
able. Also *Dasein* is usually translated as 'being there' but its
meaning emerges more clearly in Pivčević's paraphrase 'the
there of Being' (Pivčević, 1970: 110), for it is the place of openness for the world and all it comprises. The extent to which we
can be open and respond to the world is the extent to which we
live authentically. From this point of view authenticity is not
being true to some hypothetical self inside ourselves, but to
existence itself.
The question is whether authenticity, as seen by existential
philosophers, can be an aim for psychotherapy. Heidegger's concept of 'Being-in-the-world', as we have seen, describes certain
aspects of Being which are conditions of existence but to which
we are able to respond freely. To deny them would mean being in
'bad faith', and so would the denial of having the freedom to
respond to them in one way or another. Thus therapy could bring
about two things: it could enable us to accept the inevitable
characteristics of existence – like our being in the body, being
with others, the necessity of choice, the certainty of death. But it
could also help us to affirm the possibility of choosing our own
specific responses to what is 'given'.
From an existential perspective, there is at the core of many
(perhaps all) psychological disturbances a conflict between the
'givens' of existence and our response to them. The ontological
aspect of the disturbance is often covered up by its ontic manifestations. Whatever our specific explanations of compulsive
behaviour, for example, it is ontologically a bid for absolute
security in the face of Being's inevitable insecurity. The infinite
number of ways in which we shape and misshape our relationships, to give another example, needs to be understood in the light
of the fact that all existence is ontologically existence with others.

We cannot choose not to be with others - even in isolation we are still isolated from others - but we can choose *how* to be with others.

Inauthenticity is our denial of the 'given' as well as our denial of the freedom to meet it. This means, of course, that we tend to live inauthentically a great deal of the time. But at times this denial of the 'given' and of freedom, which between them encompass existence, has disturbing and even destructive consequences that bring us into therapy.

A task still to be undertaken is to establish a detailed connection between inauthenticity and particular forms of psychological disturbance. In the following I can only sketch out a few areas of existential 'givens' (Heidegger's 'existentials') and the way in which our denial of what we experience as their demands and threats can lead to disturbances.

First, what we call the 'givens' of existence, Heidegger calls our 'thrownness' into the world, into circumstances and conditions we do not choose and cannot control. Thus, we do not choose the place where we are born, our parents, the circumstances of our life. If these unchosen circumstances remain unacknowledged and denied, or if they are allowed to control us so that no choice seems left to us, we will develop a number of attitudes we could call inauthentic - idealization, resentment, confusion, a feeling of paralysis.

Second, an existential-phenomenological approach defines existence as relational. We are always in the world with others. The relational field is beset with pitfalls and clouded with anxiety: the temptation to escape into apartness and isolation is great. We can either deny relatedness altogether, or we can see it as a prison from which we can only escape into distraction and addiction. Relational difficulties of various kinds reflect this conflict with an unavoidable aspect of Being.

Third, the certainty of death is perhaps the most unacceptable dimension of existence. What is intolerable is not only the constant threat of our mortality but also the acceptance of our finiteness. We do not wish to give up our illusions of omnipotence or our hope of immortality. We may extend these attitudes to any kind of separation or loss. To live as if we were immortal, to ignore separation, to refuse to mourn our losses, are all poignant instances of living inauthentically.

Thus if we define authenticity as an openness to existence, an acceptance of what is 'given' as well as our freedom to respond to it, a more authentic way of living can, in my view, be seen as an aim of psychotherapy. However, all forms of psychotherapy have a tendency to set norms; to assume more or less explicitly what is healthy and ill, mature and immature, true and false. Existential therapy is not free from this tendency, and it is important that 'authentic' and 'inauthentic' do not become yet another measure of psychological 'wholeness'. E. van Deurzen-Smith points out that 'authenticity' is a 'much abused term, which misleadingly suggests that there is a true self, whereas the existential view is that self is relationship and process' (1996b: 174).

Heidegger denied strongly that inauthenticity is, so to speak, the 'night view' of existence. 'We would misunderstand the ontologico-existential structure of falling [inauthenticity] if we came to ascribe to it the sense of a bad and deplorable ontic property of which, perhaps, more advanced stages of human culture might be able to rid themselves' (Heidegger, 1962: 220). In other words, our conflict with what is given and our reluctance to accept our freedom are intrinsic aspects of our existence.

It cannot be the therapist's task to judge the degree of a client's authenticity. However, if the client's distress indicates that it may be rooted in a conflict with unavoidable aspects of existence itself or in the paralysing feeling that he or she has neither choice nor responsibility, the therapist can attempt to open up the ontological dimension pervading the ontic manifestations of the conflict. This may lead the client to a new understanding and the possibility of a new response. But in the end it is the client who determines the aim of psychotherapy.

References

Cannon, B. (1991) *Sartre and Psychoanalysis. An Existential Challenge to Clinical Metatheory*. Kansas: University Press of Kansas.

Deurzen-Smith, E. van (1996a) 'The survival of the self', *Journal of the Society for Existential Analysis*, 7(1): 56–66.

Deurzen-Smith, E. van (1996b) 'Existential therapy', in W. Dryden (ed.), *Handbook of Individual Therapy*. London: Sage Publications.

Heidegger, M. (1962) *Being and Time*. Tr. J. Macquarrie and E. Robinson. Oxford: Blackwell.

Heidegger, M. (1987) *Zollikoner Seminaire. Protokolle – Gespräche – Briefe*. Ed. M. Boss. Frankfurt a.M.: Klostermann.

Laing, R.D. (1960) *The Divided Self. An Existential Study in Sanity and Madness*. Harmondsworth: Penguin Books.

Pivčević, E. (1970) *Husserl and Phenomenology*. London: Hutchinson.

Rycroft, C. (1995) *A Critical Dictionary of Psychoanalysis*. 2nd edn. Harmondsworth: Penguin Books.

Sartre, J-P. (1958) *Being and Nothingness. An Essay on Phenomenological Ontology*. Tr. H. Barnes. London: Methuen.

Winnicott, D.W. (1965) *The Maturational Processes and the Facilitating Environment*. London: Hogarth Press.

Recommended Reading

Binswanger, L. (1963) *Being-in-the-World. Selected Papers.* Tr. J. Needleman. New York: Basic Books.

Boss, M. (1963) *Psychoanalysis and Daseinsanalysis.* Tr. L.B. Lefebre. New York: Basic Books.

Boss, M. (1979) *Existential Foundations of Medicine and Psychology.* Tr. S. Conway and A. Cleaves. Northvale, NJ: Jason Aronson.

Cannon, B. (1991) *Sartre and Psychoanalysis. An Existentialist Challenge to Clinical Metatheory.* Kansas: University Press of Kansas.

Cooper, D.E. (1990) *Existentialism. A Reconstruction.* Oxford: Blackwell.

Cooper, D.E. (1996) *Heidegger.* London: Claridge Press.

Crossley, N. (1996) *Intersubjectivity. The Fabric of Social Becoming.* London: Sage Publications.

Deurzen-Smith, E. van (1988) *Existential Counselling in Practice.* London: Sage Publications.

Deurzen-Smith, E. van (1996) 'Existential therapy', in W. Dryden (ed.), *Individual Therapy.* London: Sage Publications.

Deurzen-Smith, E. van (1996) *Everyday Mysteries. Existential Dimensions of Psychotherapy.* London: Routledge.

Freud, S. (1986) *The Essentials of Psycho-Analysis.* Selected, with an introduction and commentaries by Anna Freud. Penguin Books: Harmondsworth.

Friedman, M. (ed.) (1991) *Worlds of Existentialism. A Critical Reader.* New Jersey: Humanities Press.

Hammond, S.M., Howarth, J. and Keat, R. (1991) *Understanding Phenomenology.* Oxford: Blackwell.

Heidegger, M. (1962) *Being and Time.* Tr. J. Macquarrie and E. Robinson. Oxford: Blackwell.

Heidegger, M. (1993) *Basic Writings.* Introduction D.F. Krell. London: Routledge.

May, R., Angel, E. and Ellenberger, H.F. (eds) (1958) *Existence.* New York: Basic Books.

Merleau-Ponty, M. (1962) *Phenomenology of Perception.* Tr. C. Smith. London: Routledge & Kegan Paul.

Mulhall, S. (1996) *Heidegger and Being and Time.* London: Routledge.

Pivčević, E. (1970) *Husserl and Phenomenology*. London: Hutchinson.

Sartre, J-P. (1948) *Existentialism and Humanism*. Tr. P. Mairet. London: Methuen.

Sartre, J-P. (1958) *Being and Nothingness. An Essay on Phenomenological Ontology*. Tr. H. Barnes. London: Methuen.

Solomon, R.C. (1972) *From Rationalism to Existentialism*. New York: Harper & Row.

Spiegelberg, H. (1972) *Phenomenology in Psychology and Psychiatry. A Historical Introduction*. Evanston: Northwestern University Press.

Spinelli, E. (1989) *The Interpreted World. An Introduction to Phenomenological Psychology*. London: Sage Publications.

Spinelli, E. (1994) *Demystifying Therapy*. London: Constable.

Index

Compiled by Meg Davies (Registered Indexer)

12.